INFINITE INCOME

THE EIGHT-FIGURE FORMULA
FOR YOUR ONLINE BUSINESS

INFINITE
INCOME

TANNER CHIDESTER

LIONCREST
PUBLISHING

INFINITE INCOME
The Eight-Figure Formula for Your Online Business

ISBN   978-1-5445-1816-9 *Hardcover*

978-1-5445-1815-2 *Paperback*

978-1-5445-1814-5 *Ebook*

CONTENTS

FOREWORD

BY DAVID FREY

Tanner has always had a dream of playing Division I football and going on to play in the pros. In high school he was a team captain, all district, and took his team to the Texas state semi-finals. But injuries plagued him, and after short playing stints at BYU and Arizona Western, he came back home to Friendswood, Texas, deflated but determined. You see, Tanner isn't only an exceptional athlete; he was a 4.0 student and smart as a whip. He was accepted into the prestigious petroleum engineering program at Texas A&M, which is no small feat.

I've known Tanner since he was a young kid. I was his church youth leader. I've been a full-time internet entrepreneur for twenty years, and when Tanner came back into town, I invited him to join me for lunch. I wanted to catch up with him and talk about his future. I knew that Tanner had the smarts and drive to create his own business online and work for himself. He had the looks and the body, so I believed he could make a great living as an online personal trainer.

At lunch that day, I urged him to drop out of college and become an online entrepreneur. He didn't know the first thing about internet marketing, but I knew he was smart (but I never realized just how smart he was till later on). I offered him a desk in my office and personal mentoring.

I'll never forget the day that Texas A&M's admissions office called him to finalize his acceptance to their petroleum engineering program. He put them on hold, looked at me and asked, "Should I do it?" I looked right back at him and said, "Yes. Do it." So he got back on the phone and told them he wouldn't be coming to school that year. After he hung up the phone, I think he was a little stunned at what he had just done. I told him, "I'm proud of you. You just burned the ship. You'll remember this day for the rest of your life." So for the next year, Tanner would show up in my office every day, ready to learn and work.

There was one problem: Tanner was broke. He drove an old, butt-ugly Mazda Protege that had been handed down to him. He had no source of income and didn't have a dime in his pocket. So he decided to do male modeling on the side to make some money. He quickly discovered that male physique modeling was full of seedy people. Some of the pro photographers wanted him to pose totally nude because there was big money in selling his nude images to gay websites and magazines. He turned them down. But the photos they did take left little to the imagination.

Tanner was so broke and desperate to make a few bucks, he took on some of the weirdest jobs, most of which I cannot write about. But I'll give you a taste by just saying one dude paid Tanner $300 a month to receive three pairs of Tanner's dirty underwear. Ewww. Like I said, it was a seedy business, but Tanner was desperate. He didn't want to get a full-time job because that wouldn't leave him enough time to work on his business.

To keep his chiseled physique for modeling, he would eat next to nothing. I remember he would bring one can of tuna to eat every day and a gallon of water. That was about it. He was always falling asleep in his chair from exhaustion. Sometimes, I would snap photos and videos of him sleeping and post them on Facebook just to have some fun. He became known as my "sleepy intern." Tanner was working out so hard and eating so little that there were days he would literally come into the office, lie down on the floor, and go to sleep. One time he decided to have a cheat meal so I took him to an all-you-can-eat salad buffet. He was so hungry that I swear he ate half of the salad bar!

If I had to label Tanner with one word, I would use the word "determined." Tanner had more drive to succeed than anyone I'd ever met. He would get up at 4:30 a.m. and go to bed at 11:00 p.m. and work all in between (except for the naps). He was too broke to date and was embarrassed to pick up a girl in his run-down Mazda Protege. So he put all his energy into his business.

After a year of working in my office, he still wasn't making any money to speak of. He built out a great product but didn't have any money to promote it. So he decided to move to Utah to get a part-time job as a server. It wasn't glorious, but it allowed him to survive and still work on his business. He moved to L.A. for a little while and worked as a food delivery boy. He spent more money paying parking fines than he made from delivering food. He got a few paid modeling gigs here and there, but nothing to speak of. I remember a couple of times he called me up so depressed, he talked about maybe quitting. But I knew he could make it if he just kept trying. I believed in him and his ability to find success. I urged him to keep working side jobs and continue learning and studying how to get fitness training clients.

He then got a commission-only job selling alarm systems in Alabama. It was there that he discovered his talent for selling. Tanner could sell. He was bold, didn't take "no" for an answer, and hustled all day street selling, all the while never giving up his dream to have his own online training business. He instantly became one of the company's top salespeople.

One day he came across a "guru" online who was selling a $5,000 coaching program promising to show you how to make a six-figure income as an online trainer. Tanner figured he could skip all the painful and time-taking "learn on your own" effort and just pay someone to learn how to get where he wanted to go. So Tanner scraped together every cent he had and invested in the program. He discovered he could take his street selling skills to the telephone and get people to agree to pay him a lot of money for fitness training. Finally he started making decent money. So he decided to quit his street selling job, move back to Texas, and go all in on his fitness training business.

In very short order, I saw Tanner turn his telephone and Instagram account into an ATM. He was so successful selling online fitness training that he started teaching others how to do it. Within one year, he had a million-dollar business doing fitness training and teaching trainers how to start their online training business.

By the way, he was running a million-dollar-a-year business out of his tiny bedroom in his parents' home. One thing about Tanner: He loves his family. He has six brothers and sisters, and he loves them all. In fact, his two younger brothers work with him in the business. Benson is his chief business and fitness coach, and Gentry was one of his fitness coaches and is his primary salesperson. Tanner's dad is a teacher, and his mom is a stay-at-home parent. They grew up on a teacher's income, and so Tanner and his brothers learned how to work for everything they wanted. There were no shortcuts in Tanner's home.

With the rise of Tanner's success, he started hiring expensive business coaches and joining high-ticket masterminds to learn how to scale his business to the next level. He learned some from most, and none from some. I remember recommending one of my friends who was promising people that he could teach them how to make six figures in thirty days with a Facebook group. The cost of the coaching program was $5,000. I trusted this person. He was successful, so I recommended him. In the end, he did zero for Tanner, and I was ashamed that I had referred Tanner to him. And my friend refused to give Tanner a refund of any kind. It was shameful. But Tanner took his financial licking and moved on. Little did Tanner know, he was in for a breakthrough in his business.

There were two things that changed everything for Tanner. The first was running online ads, which is super scary when you first start. He was barely making any money running ads and was nervous about continuing it. So out of necessity, he started following up with people who didn't sign up with him. He couldn't afford not to. And almost overnight, he started closing people right and left and literally 12X'ed his ad spend. It was a eureka moment for Tanner. I remember him coming into the gym that morning freaking out about his results from just following up with people. So Tanner worked hard to perfect the follow-up process that had brought him so much success. And he started building out a team of people to help him do it.

Fast-forward one year, and Tanner "tentupled" his business. He went from doing one million a year to generating revenues of over ten million dollars a year! That's almost unheard of in the coaching industry. He then replicated his marketing process and started offering it to other types of coaches and consultants. Today, he is the King Kong of his market. He is one of the top business coaches in the world because he never gave up. He's built out a team of forty people, and now he can go anywhere he wants, buy anything he wants, financially help anyone he wants, and do just about anything he wants. He's gone from sleeping on my office floor to living in a 6,000-square-foot high-rise penthouse on Miami Beach and driving a custom Lamborghini in less than three years.

What sets Tanner apart from most other aspiring entrepreneurs is that he has an untiring work ethic and a "never give up" attitude. He probably learned that from his time playing football. He is humble enough to know he doesn't know everything, so he's an insatiable learner. He has more drive and determination to succeed in his pinkie than most have in their whole body. He has an uncanny ability and boldness to network with the most influential people. And he has no fear. He had the boldness and courage to spend his last dollar on advertising and coaching programs. In fact, Tanner has spent more money on coaching and mentoring than anyone I know in my twenty years of online marketing. That's why Tanner can charge people $10k, $20k, and even $50k for his advice and coaching without batting an eye. He's been in the shoes of most everyone who is considering buying coaching from him. He knows what it feels like to spend the only money you have on reaching your dream. He's done it. He has the stripes on his back to prove it.

In this book, you'll learn the nitty-gritty of how Tanner makes his fortune. Millions of dollars in wisdom and experience are wrapped up in this book. He charges clients tens of thousands of dollars for what you're about to learn inside its pages, so don't take it lightly. This book can be a gift that keeps on giving or a coaster to set your drinks on. The decision is yours as to whether you'll implement what Tanner teaches you in this book. The spoils go to those who implement and never give up.

INTRODUCTION

If you had unlimited money, what would you do with your time?

If you're like most people, you currently spend a lot of your life solving day-to-day problems, such as paying bills, fixing leaks, and figuring out how to finance things. You're making just enough money to get by, and you're typically working a nine-to-five job. You're tired of working hard and going in circles and not getting the results you want from your life.

Even if you have a good lifestyle—let's say you're making $100,000 a year—you're not really able to travel because you don't get a lot of vacation time, you have obligations at work, and you have to answer to someone (your boss). To make matters worse, you don't really like your job and your boss is a jerk. Sure, you're making decent money, but your schedule is not your own. There's also a cap on your income, so it hinders your ability to retire or do what you want, when you want, because you only have so much money to spend.

Life becomes monotonous—you wake up, you go to school, you graduate, you get a job, get married, have kids, and then you die (depressing to think about, I know, but that's the reality for most people). Once you've entered the rat race, you go to work, come home, go to work, come home, take a two-week vacation each year, and repeat until you can retire.

In a perfect world, most people would like to do what they want when they want. Some would like to travel, others would like to live off the grid, and many would like time to pursue a hobby, learn a new language or instrument, or simply have more time to spend with their family and take better care of themselves. They don't like someone telling them what they can or can't do.

They want more control.

The only way to get out of a nine-to-five job and to have control, to live a lifestyle where you are financially secure or carefree, is to start your own business—and in today's climate, an online business is one of the best options. When you own your own business and make a lot of money, you can do what you want, when you want, and with whom you want. And when it's all said and done, happiness is about connecting with and giving back to others. It's hard to do that when you don't control your schedule or income.

The people who ask me to help them build a successful online business all desire different lifestyles, but they also seek one common thing: freedom. I wanted freedom from the nine-to-five grind too. My bigger goal when I began building my online business was to use my time and money for good—I like to think others starting a business share this goal too.

In order to create the lifestyle I have today, with unlimited earning potential and plenty of free time to do the things I love outside of work, I asked myself the same question I asked you earlier: If I had unlimited money, what would I do with my time?

That question and my responses led me to start an online business and grow revenue to $10 million-plus per year in less than two years.

Starting an online business can change your life like it did mine.

But before I teach you how to change your life with an online business, let me tell you how I went from being a bullied youth to becoming a highly successful online business owner.

ZERO TO HERO

I grew up in a family of seven kids. We were a very sheltered, religious Mormon household. To this day, my dad is a teacher who's also heavily involved in the church, and I'm proud of him for it. While religion and politics are not exactly my cup of tea, I got my drive and work ethic from my father, and I'm forever grateful to him. Growing up, we didn't have a lot of money. I don't want to make it sound worse than it was; I always had what I needed, but that was it. I distinctly remember asking my father for money to go to the movies when I was fourteen years old. His response was "Well, you don't have a job, so guess not." At the time it upset me, but it gave me the inner fuel I needed to become successful. When I was younger, I didn't have many friends, and the only people I had to play with were my two older sisters. I think I was kind of weird compared to the other kids in school because of my family situation. Dress-up and tea parties with sisters can do that to you.

When I got to sixth grade, I finally realized the other kids were making fun of me. That really made me sad, hurt, and angry, and I would go home crying to my parents. I didn't understand why people were so mean for no reason. This pattern repeated for a while until I realized that my parents couldn't help me and that I had to help myself if I wanted things to change. That's when I started working out. My intent was to become super muscular so I could force the bullies to stop picking on me. It worked, and as a result,

I built a lot of confidence, excelled in school and sports, became captain of the football team, and received several small college football scholarship offers.

I dreamed of playing in the NFL. But after multiple back-to-back labrum surgeries due to injuries, I realized I had no chance of making it to the NFL. I also played with top-five draft pick Ezekiel Ansah, a genetic phenom from Ghana who played a total of six college games before being picked fifth in the draft. I realized no matter how hard I tried, I could never beat a guy of his potential. Furthermore, football was taking a physical toll. I was tired of doing six-month rehabs on my shoulder only to get hurt again, so I stopped playing.

Transferring colleges twice—first from Brigham Young University to Arizona Western, then from Arizona Western to Texas A&M—led me on a new path. I had been studying petroleum engineering but quickly realized I hated school and had only been attending college to play football. My mentor, a highly successful businessman and a family friend who I trusted and who I had met prior to starting my first semester at Texas A&M, convinced me to drop out of college to start my own business and offered to show me how. My parents, my family, and my girlfriend told me I was an idiot, literally.

But a nine-to-five job didn't appeal to me. The idea of graduating college at twenty-two and doing the same thing every day for the rest of my life sounded horrible: go into the office from nine to five and make decent money, but not great money. It was depressing. I couldn't believe this was what people called "life." It wasn't what I wanted. The only way I knew to have the lifestyle I wanted—the cars, the house, being able to help take care of my family (one of my biggest priorities)—was to make a lot of money. And the best way I saw to do that was to start an online business.

For the next two years, I learned how to run an online business from my mentor, David Frey. Creating an online business that focused on the fitness and diet industry made perfect sense. I was familiar with the fitness industry after working out for so many years, and I knew how to lose weight through diet and exercise, both from playing football and from modeling after I gave up football. The only other thing I needed was a personal trainer certification, which I quickly obtained. However, I didn't make any money as a result of working with David, at least in the beginning. Door-to-door sales, modeling, and working as a server paid my bills. At the time I felt like a failure, but everything David was teaching me and what I was learning on the sales job prepared me for financial explosion.

When I turned twenty-five, my business wasn't going anywhere and I needed a change. Desperate to find success, I was willing to do anything, including spending my last dollar.

That's when I finally hired a coach (charging more than half of the $5,000 fee to my credit card because I didn't have enough money in the bank to cover the cost) and started making money online. The first twelve months in business, I made over a million dollars in revenue and received a Two Comma Club Award (for making $1,000,000 in revenue) as a result of using ClickFunnels, a marketing tool that got my name out into the fitness industry. Soon, fitness trainers asked me for help to grow their online businesses because they wanted to make more money too. I started another business to fill this need and hit seven figures of income within three months. Seven months ago, I branched out even further and started a new business to help general business owners increase their online business income, which has further exploded my top-line revenue.

Fast-forward to today: I'm twenty-eight, my business generates over $10 million annually in revenue (on pace for $15 million this year), and I employ over forty people. In only two years, I built an eight-figure online business (from the time I started making money until today).

A PROVEN ROADMAP TO SUCCESS

I've figured out the process to help someone who has little skill, no money, and no experience build a successful online business. Like anything in life, nothing is 100 percent foolproof, but the process and methods I teach give online business owners the greatest chance of success. A coach's job is to do just that: give his students the easiest path with the highest chance of success possible. That doesn't mean they won't have to work hard or learn skills to be successful. It does mean they will know the best strategy to succeed.

Business is like baseball. You can't keep your foot on first base and also get to second base. You have to get off first and run. But there's a right way to run and a wrong way to run. If you run the right way, you reach second base and then third, and then maybe home plate. But if you run into the outfield, you make your life worse, not better. It's important to have success early on—to reach the next base—because the longer you go without success, the more you start doubting yourself. Ultimately, you get discouraged and then quit, never finding success because you followed the wrong path and didn't run from first to second correctly, let alone making it across home plate.

I know what it's like to almost quit. I almost quit five times over the first two years I was in business. I think 99 percent of people would have quit if they were in the same situation.

I was running the wrong way.

Until I wasn't anymore.

That's why it's so important for me to help others achieve

success with their online businesses. I have a "strong mindset" and I almost quit. I can only imagine how difficult it is for others to keep working toward their goals, especially those who don't have a support system in place.

My goal with new clients is to teach them how to run the right way so they make $10,000 minimum in the first thirty days with their online business. By making calculated decisions and mitigating risk, my clients find success faster, don't waste effort and money, and don't quit.

IT TAKES HARD WORK TO BE SUPER SUCCESSFUL

Like anything in life, if you're going to be super successful, it takes a lot of hard work.

So many people work hard and don't make any money. They try to dig a hole with a piece of paper instead of a shovel. If you dig a hole with a shovel, it's hard. But the shovel is the right tool. If you try to dig that same hole with a piece of paper, you're not going to make much progress. In order to be successful, you need to have the right process, go in the right direction, use the right tool, and work hard.

Do you want to stop working hard while not getting anywhere?

Do you want your online business to be a huge success?

There are a million different business models, a million different ways to run a business. But based on my experience and success, the business model I use and teach is the best business model for beginners. It has the highest upside and the least amount of risk. There's no upfront money, there's no skill set needed, and you can learn it from scratch in the pages of this book.

What are you waiting for?

Let's discuss the three personal tools for success that you need to understand and utilize in order to build a successful online business.

PART I

PERSONAL TOOLS FOR SUCCESS

CHAPTER I

CONFIDENCE COMES FROM ACTION

Kids can be mean, and as I stated earlier, I was picked on a lot when I was a child. The kids at school would call me Norman Mormon, Storming Mormon,[1] or Titty Chiddy (because of my last name). They'd also push me for no reason, make jokes about my religion, and embarrass me in front of girls or in class, saying things like "Why are you so freaking like Tanner? He's just a stupid Mormon." I was the butt of all their jokes—always. And it hurt. A lot. It was freaking traumatizing; at times I didn't want to go to school and would stay home. The teasing totally destroyed my confidence.

---

[1] I don't think they actually cared that I was Mormon, but my religion gave them an easy excuse to make fun of me. My Jewish friends were picked on too. It was the same for those who were short, fat, etc.—simply a way to push our buttons.

At home I'd cry and pray to God that the kids would stop being mean. My prayers went unanswered, and they kept making fun of me, day after day.

Sometimes the kids would trick me by telling me a girl liked me and that I should talk to her. I fell for it every time. For instance, when I was twelve, the other kids convinced me that a girl in class, Erica, liked me, so I bought her a big teddy bear for Valentine's Day and put it in her desk (I told my dad it was for my teacher, so he made an exception and gave me the money). I thought she'd be surprised and happy when she saw it, but she simply said, "Thanks." Her lack of enthusiasm and slight embarrassment told me she didn't really want it. Her friends and most of the class started laughing and said Erica was being nice because she felt bad for me. That afternoon the teddy bear sat next to the driver on the school bus. When I asked him how he got it, he said Erica gave it to him. I was so angry. So demoralized. I went home and played video games because I didn't know what else to do.

Even though Erica gave away the bear, she was super nice to me in the days, weeks, and months to come. And it wasn't because she felt bad for me. She was being nice because that's who she is. Most people are only nice to you when you have something to offer or to give them. At that time, I had nothing to offer and was an oddball. Erica was one of the most popular girls in school, but she still treated me as an equal, unlike the other popular girls who were mean. When I became older and more popular, all the mean girls started being nice to me, but I knew they only were acting that way because I had become popular.

As the years progressed, Erica and I became closer and closer, and now Erica's one of my best friends. If more people were like Erica, the world would be a better place.

Another time that same year, the guys on my Peewee football team laughed at me and hit me after practice because I was an easy target. Crying, I went home and told my dad what had happened. He said, "Son, you know I can talk to you about it and try to help you. But ultimately, if you're going to come home crying every day, maybe you shouldn't play football." That was when I realized my dad couldn't help me and it was up to me to change if I wanted the bullying to stop.

Refusing to quit football and determined to improve my life, I turned to weight lifting. My thought was that if I got big and beat those kids up, they would stop picking on me.

On the way to Bible study at 5:30 a.m. every day with my sisters, my mom dropped me off at the twenty-four-hour fitness center by our house (my parents paid the $10 per month membership fee because they supported any activity that they believed would be good for me). It was painful to lift weights at first because I'd never lifted. My muscles were so sore, but I kept working out, starting with low weights and steadily increasing the pounds. Soon, my body acclimated, and I grew muscle rapidly. After three months of consistent work—it was the hardest thing I'd done in my life at the time—I'd made a lot of progress. Guys who used to tease me started complimenting me, saying things like "Dude, you're getting huge." Girls would say, "Tanner, are you working out?" That was the first time in my life kids said nice things to me. Their compliments and noticing positive things about me boosted my confidence, and I strove to work even harder.

The more compliments I received, the more my confidence increased. As my confidence increased, I began to behave differently. I went from being timid, shy, and embarrassed to being assertive and thinking I was the big man on campus.

If someone still dared to make fun of me, I threatened to beat him up. The kid's friends would say things like "Tanner will. He's big. He's going to kick your ass." That switched the narrative from "Hey, let's make fun of Tanner" to "Tanner's a badass. He's going to beat you up. You shouldn't mess with him." And no one did.

I saw my hard work in the gym paying off and realized that if I put the same hard work into school and sports, I would see positive results. Soon, my grades improved, and I started getting straight A's. Girls started talking to me (even the girls who had made fun of me in the past), and I felt confident talking to them too. The following year, in seventh grade, I moved up from the Peewee football team to becoming one of the best players on the school's traveling team. Football is big in Texas, where I grew up, so being a great football player gives you a lot of clout.

Going through the process from being picked on and feeling insecure and embarrassed to being a hardworking individual who feels confident made me realize that if I wanted good things to happen in my life, all I needed to do was set a goal and work hard. That's what propelled me to become successful at a young age—I knew I could accomplish whatever I wanted.

TAKE ACTION

As you can see by my story, you can't become successful by praying for change, like most people wish they could. Nothing changes until you take action, and those actions lead to new results. Taking action requires effort; however, success only happens when you take action.

Once you take action, others will provide feedback. That's where fear comes in because you won't know what kind of feedback to expect. You'll feel uncomfortable. But only by listening to feedback will you know you took the right action—or if you need to take a different action.

It's like putting your hand on the stove. If the stove is hot and you don't do anything except look at it, nothing happens (no action, nothing changes). But if you touch the stove (take action) and burn your fingers (feedback), you learn not to do that again (new result). The same principle applies to business. You won't know if an action is the correct action until you take it and receive feedback. But you must take action, fight for what you want, and tolerate the fear of the unknown, or nothing in your life will change. Trust that eventually you will figure out the right actions if you keep trying.

When starting my business, I figured it out as I went. The more actions I took, the more feedback I received. If something didn't work, I did something else instead. I was willing to make mistakes because those mistakes would give me the guidance I needed to succeed.

Once you reach a place where "it can't get any worse," that's when you truly become empowered. I remember when I had thought, "I'd rather be homeless than unsuccessful another second," and I meant it. That's when I truly had no fear anymore because I knew that being unsuccessful was the worst thing that could happen to me—it was only uphill from there.

Most people are scared to make mistakes. They don't want to fail. But you can't be afraid of making mistakes because every time you make a mistake, it brings you closer to your goal.

So how do you get to your goal? You reverse engineer it.

REVERSE ENGINEERING AND WHY IT'S IMPORTANT

Reverse engineering is figuring out how to achieve a goal by starting with the goal and going through the steps it will take to get there in reverse order. For example, if you want to run a marathon, start with the final goal in mind (running the marathon) and work backward, identifying each step you need to achieve along the way to reach your goal (keep reading to see examples of how to reverse engineer).

Most people don't reach their goals for one of two reasons:

1. The goal is not specific and measurable. Saying you want to make more money or be happier is an arbitrary goal. How much more money do you want to make? $1,000? A million? Or if you want to be happier, how will you know if you've hit your goal? Do you feel better for a day? A week? Have a girlfriend? By making your goal specific and measurable, you either hit the goal or you don't. You either succeed or fail.
2. They identify a goal but don't plan how to get there. Reverse engineering gives you the steps you need to

take to make hitting your goal predictable. It removes the uncertainty from the process, which is what people typically fear the most and what keeps them from being successful.

Having a specific and measurable goal and a reverse engineered plan to get to the goal prevents you from going in five hundred different directions and not going anywhere. Each goal has unique steps. It's important to know your goal so you can take the proper steps to reach it.

Don't be afraid to think big. Instead of determining any old goal, determine your biggest goal.

DETERMINING YOUR BIGGEST GOAL

You're probably wondering: What's the difference between a goal and my biggest goal? Your biggest goal is what you want to achieve more than anything else. For example, if you want to become a billionaire, don't make it your goal to become a millionaire—that's just a milestone you reach along the way. Pick your biggest goal and work backward from there—it gives you the greatest chance of success.

Determining your biggest goal also will inform the things you do to reach it. For example, if I'm currently making $10 million a year with my business and my goal is to make $25 million, I need a different business model or I won't reach my goal. Knowing my biggest goal gives me the starting point—or end point—to reverse engineer the process so I can achieve it.

What's your biggest goal? Think about it; write it down. Now make it bigger. I'm guessing it's still not big enough, so try again. This is between you and you, so don't sell yourself short. Write down your truly biggest goal. Also write down why it's important for you to achieve it.

Now that you know your biggest goal and your motivation to achieve it, you must determine what you want to happen.

DETERMINING WHAT YOU WANT TO HAPPEN

As we discussed, you must take steps to reach your goal. That involves determining what you want to happen. If my biggest goal is that I don't want to be bullied, for example, what I want to happen is to be able to beat up people if they don't leave me alone. In order to achieve that goal, the reverse engineered steps I must take are:

1. I want to be able to beat people up: How do I do that?
2. Gain muscle: How do I do that?
3. Lift weights: When and where can I do that?
4. At the gym early in the morning: How do I make that happen?
5. Get up earlier than usual.

If you're struggling with your online business (or want to start one) and your biggest goal is to make a certain amount of money—let's say $10,000 a month—what do you want to happen?

1. You want to convert those you speak with on the phone calls into clients: How do you do that?
2. You have to convince potential clients to talk to you on the phone: How do you find those people?
3. You get leads (someone who is interested in your offer) and follow up on those leads: How do you get leads?
4. You hire a coach who shows you how to get them.

The more you engage in the process of obtaining leads and converting them into clients, the more money you make.

Knowing your biggest goal and what you want to happen is not enough to achieve success. You also must know how to execute the goal.

HOW TO EXECUTE THE GOAL

Two of my clients, Tikis and Amanda, are fitness trainers who own an online business that helps people get in shape and lose weight. By the time they came to me, they had already spent a lot of money and about two and a half years working with various business coaches. Although Tikis and Amanda followed the coaches' advice, they did not achieve the results they desired and were afraid they would have to close their online business and return to working nine-to-five-jobs, which they didn't want to do.

Tikis and Amanda's biggest goal was to make at least $10,000 in sales per month. To execute their goal, they needed four clients at $2,500 every month. To close that number of clients, they needed one hundred qualified leads. To get one hundred qualified leads, they had to get their business message in front of one thousand people. Leads are important because they turn into sales phone calls, which ultimately turn into sales, which turn into paying clients. Leads can be obtained organically or through paid ads on social media platforms, such as Facebook and Instagram. Yet most business owners fail from the start because they don't know how to get their message out.

I taught Tikis and Amanda not only how to obtain consistent leads but how to convert them into a sales phone call and ultimately into paying clients. It's easier said than done, like anything in life. I also taught them how to sell high-ticket deals, typically between $1,500 and $6,000 for a four-month program.

Once Tikis and Amanda implemented what I taught them (executed their goal), they consistently made sales. In a short time, they were making $10,000-plus per month.

It's important to know that if Tikis and Amanda decide they want to execute a new goal (making $30,000 per month, for example), they will need to step back and reverse engineer the process again. A new goal requires a change in direction and therefore different processes.

HOW EXECUTING A GOAL LEADS TO CONFIDENCE

When you try something and it works, it reinforces your confidence. But you have to first identify what action you're going to try. People often hire coaches because they don't know what they need to do in order to become successful or, even if they know the actions to take, they're not confident in their skills.

When Tikis and Amanda came to me, their business wasn't making money because they weren't making sales. They weren't making sales because they didn't know how to obtain leads and close sales on the phone. We worked together to build those skills necessary to execute their goal.

Once Tikis and Amanda executed their goal for their online fitness business, they constantly texted me and sent me screenshots of their success. Their confidence soared as they saw the results of their efforts. They were making a lot of sales, which allowed them to pay their bills and afford a nice place to live. They were excited about their online business and no longer worried about being forced to return to working nine-to-five jobs. Now they work from home, work the hours they want, and make multiple six figures a year in income.

The positive reinforcement you receive—as a result of obtaining positive results—leads to confidence, which in turn makes it easier to achieve continued success. Increasing your confidence changes your life from one that is governed by chance to one that is predicable.

GOING FROM "LIFE IS CHANCE" TO "LIFE IS PREDICTABLE"

Many people think that success is chance. That's not true. They just don't know how to set a goal and do what it takes to reach it. When you set a goal and write down each step you need to take to reach that goal, you're not guessing. You know that if you do the required work and take each step you've identified, you will hit your goal. That is not chance; that is predictability.

Knowing your numbers and averages is important in life and in sales. For example, if a guy uses the dating app Tinder and swipes right one hundred times, maybe fifty girls will respond. Ten of those fifty girls will show up in person to a date. Out of those ten, three will be enjoyable to hang out with, and out of those three, you pick a girl to continue dating.

The first time you try something, track the numbers to see what they are. After that, you know what you need to do to achieve your desired results. So, based on the preceding example, if you want to find three girls who are enjoyable to hang out with, you need to swipe right one hundred times on Tinder.

My life feels predictable because every time I set a goal, I reverse engineer the goal to figure out what I need to do to reach it. Then I take the required steps, I get results, and I'm happy. I've done that with everything I've ever wanted to achieve: not being bullied, getting girls, making more money, living in a penthouse in Miami, etc. I don't feel like there's anything I can't do.

WHEN REVERSE ENGINEERING DOESN'T WORK

Reverse engineering doesn't work for one of two reasons: poor execution or poor skill level. Here are some examples:

1. You want to lose fifty pounds. You work out every day, but you eat a Big Mac before bed every night. You get angry because you're not losing weight. You're not doing what you're supposed to be doing—not eating those Big Macs every night (poor execution—you know what food to avoid, but you're eating it anyway).
2. You're running an online business. You message one hundred people on social media but say weird things

in your messages. People think you're weird and ignore you. You're not sending the right message to make sales (poor skill level—you don't know how to send the proper message, but you can learn).

You might be asking yourself: If I reverse engineer my biggest goal and take all the steps to make it happen, will it work 100 percent of the time? Yes, with the exception of skill level. For example, anyone can play basketball, but not everyone can play in the NBA. It's not because basketball is a hard game. It's because professional basketball players have a different skill level than the rest of us (in addition to their innate physical attributes). A business coach can help you improve poor skill levels, much like a basketball player can improve his skill level if he has a good coach.

Your experience is probably different than mine; everyone's experience is different because each of us takes a different path to our goals, even if the goals are the same. But it's almost impossible to have success if you don't take action (and tolerate any discomfort it may cause). You need the proper skill plus the proper path, combined with execution, in order to achieve success.

Stop thinking life is chance and luck. Believe you can do what you want if you take the necessary steps and correct actions to make changes. Know that as you take those actions and begin to experience success, your confidence will grow, driving you to take more actions leading to more confidence and success.

You're going to make mistakes along the way, but as long as you're committed to achieving your biggest goal and you're willing to learn from your mistakes and increase your skill level (that's where a coach comes in), you will be successful.

Taking action leads to encountering roadblocks along your path to success, and you need to know how to deal with them.

CHAPTER 2

WORKING HARD AND WEATHERING DIFFICULTIES

As I stated earlier, I began to work out and lift weights when I was twelve years old and in the sixth grade. Soon, I bulked up and joined a Peewee football team. However, I wasn't very good because I lacked confidence after being bullied for so long and being told I was stupid all the time. But I kept working out and playing football, and as the days progressed and I saw my skills improve, I gained more and more confidence. After a while, I didn't care what people said to me. That's what confidence really is: not being affected by someone else's words. It's knowing your own worth, knowing you are good at what you do and that the other person is the one who has issues.

In junior high school, I was one of the best players on the football team. In high school, my goal was to make the varsity team as a sophomore, so ninth grade was a pretty big year for me. I didn't care how my season turned out. I was more concerned about the coaches who were watching the younger players to see who performed and who could play well. It was my chance to show that I could excel at the varsity level. As I stated earlier, football's everything in Texas, where I grew up, so I wanted to be the best I could be. If you make varsity as a sophomore, essentially you're a badass. And that's what I wanted.

I had a killer freshman season and the coaches loved me. They also liked that I spent a lot of time in the weight room—I always worked out in a spot that allowed them to see me and my dedication. I made the varsity football team my sophomore year, one of only three sophomores to do so. In my junior year, I had an incredible season—making the all-district and all-county teams—and my school team went to the state semifinals. Prior to that season, we never made it past the first round of the finals. Unfortunately, I broke my ankle during the last game.

Mid-season senior year, my shoulders began hurting a lot. I didn't know why, and I didn't do anything about it. I was determined to keep playing football despite the pain—that was my mentality. We had another really good season but lost in the quarterfinals.

I received a couple of scholarship offers, including one from Nicholls State, a smaller Division I football team; however, it was pulled due to a coaching staff change as I was getting ready to attend. Once I lost that opportunity, my parents wanted me to attend Brigham Young University because I grew up Mormon, so I enrolled and became a walk-on football player.

When my shoulders started hurting again, an MRI revealed that most of the ligaments in both shoulders were completely torn. I kept playing football, but whenever I would hit someone, my bones would collide. It was super painful and I couldn't keep playing. Two shoulder surgeries followed, along with a six-month rehab period for each.

Brigham Young University was fine, but I didn't really like the school overall. It had nothing to do with football, just the school in general, so I transferred to Arizona Western College on a scholarship. Arizona Western is one of the top football junior colleges that sends a lot of football players to prestigious Division I schools and to the NFL. My goal was to prove I could stay healthy, transfer and play football at a school like Texas A&M University, and ultimately play in the NFL.

At Arizona Western, I hurt my shoulder again during my first football practice. That led to a third surgery and another six months of rehab. At that point, I made the difficult decision to give it all up.

I was done. Football wasn't going to work out for me. I couldn't stay healthy. The NFL was not going to invest in someone who got hurt that much, and that's assuming I'd even be drafted.

For those who are unaware, the NFL draft is similar to when captains pick teams for recreational sports. All thirty-two NFL teams have a list of players and select which players they want to play for them.

Only 1 percent of all collegiate athletes get picked in the NFL draft each year; it's extremely competitive.

Despite knowing I'd been the best I could be, I wasn't good enough. There was, however, a satisfaction in knowing I had given football my absolute all.

I thought my life was over. I was a football player and then suddenly I wasn't. Football had been my identity, and for the first time since sixth grade, I wasn't playing football. Not knowing what I wanted to do with my life made me feel extremely depressed, because I felt I no longer had a purpose. At the same time, I felt relief in not having to work so hard anymore.

After approximately four months, I realized I could either sit and pout for the rest of my life or move on. I brushed myself off and thought about my options. A nine-to-five job was not one I would even consider—that would make me just like everybody else. There wouldn't be anything special about me. Not that "being like everyone else" is bad, but I've always had the highest expectations for myself. So I asked myself: What else could I do? How could I become a somebody? What type of work would allow me to become successful and make a lot of money? In my mind, business was the only option. In this world, if you're a somebody, you usually make a lot of money, and you're either a celebrity, a professional athlete, or a successful businessman. That was my reality at the time, even if it may be false.

I shifted my focus from working out in the gym nine hours a day (when I played sports and didn't have school, or it was the summer) to working nine hours a day on building an online fitness business (my first business model). I wouldn't have to pay part of my profits to the gym, I could charge higher prices, I could work with more clients online than in person, and I wouldn't have to buy my own gym if I wanted to expand and make more money. I could work from anywhere in the world, and I would be my own boss and have more control over my life.

When life's obstacles prevent you from achieving your dream, the difficulties you experience, along with the hard work you put into future endeavors, will give you what you need to discover a new way to achieve success and fulfill new dreams.

SUCCESS ISN'T POSSIBLE WITHOUT FAILURE

Greatness means you're doing something that most people can't. If you're doing something most people can't, that means most people fail or don't try. In reality, everyone fails at some point. Everyone makes mistakes. If you think you won't, you're wrong. It's impossible to try to achieve something great and not mess up along the way.

I didn't become a millionaire simply because I wanted to. I made a lot of mistakes along the way because I didn't know how to avoid them. When mistakes occurred, I'd feel depressed and wonder if I'd ever figure things out. I'd ask myself: Am I doing the wrong thing? Am I following the wrong path? Am I executing things properly? Or am I just stupid?

It's important to accept that you will fail when you try new things. You will question your judgment. You will feel frustrated and upset, especially when you've done your best. But that doesn't mean you should give up. You need to redefine success.

REDEFINED SUCCESS

When you've taken a specific path as far as possible and worked as hard as you can to achieve a goal that you really want but have come to realize that it will never happen, you need to find something else that will bring you success. For example, Mark Cuban loves basketball, but he was never going to be great at basketball and play in the NBA. He understood that. He redefined success by becoming a tech genius and buying the Dallas Mavericks basketball team.

My clients redefine success all the time. They hire me when they're working nine-to-five jobs they no longer want, there's a cap on their incomes, and they want to make more money. They're tired of commuting and want to work from home or from a tropical paradise. With my help, they change paths (redefine success) and start online businesses.

One of my clients, Bo, is a super-smart, young guy. When he first began working, he defined success as many do by his income and job security. He made a six-figure income at a nine-to-five sales job—that he hated. When he came to me, he wanted more free time and a job he loved. His true passion is fitness; he became certified as a trainer and started an online fitness business. Today, he makes more money than before, works from home, and has time to travel pretty much anywhere he wants. In order for Bo to live life the way he desired, he had to redefine success, and that meant moving from sales and working for someone else to owning an online business.

LEARNING FROM FAILURES AND REDIRECTING

Most people who talk to me about their business issues are

mentally soft, like melting ice cream. They can't put up with much adversity. When bad things happen, they fall apart. They want things to be easy. They consider quitting instead of learning from their failures and redirecting their efforts.

You have two options in life: You can become a nobody or a somebody. You can be the person who walks through life, scrapes by, never goes on vacation, and barely pays the bills, or you can learn from your failures and redirect.

Bo already had the right mentality when he hired me to help him create his online business. Like a lot of sales guys who earn commissions by making sales, Bo worked hard and knew how to learn from his failures and redirect; this made him a good candidate for owning an online business.

My failures used to feel like a waste of time. I'd think I was an idiot because I couldn't figure out how to do something right the first time. I'd tell myself I was dumb. Looking back, I now know that was wrong. I needed to live with the discomfort and pain, maybe even depression, learn from my failures, and redirect my efforts toward what worked.

Success comes through failure. The more mistakes you make, the faster you become successful, but only if you learn from those mistakes and redirect. Think of a jigsaw puzzle: if you keep trying to fit different puzzle pieces into a specific spot, eventually one will fit. That's how success works—you make a mistake, try something new, and eventually find what works, unless you don't learn from your mistakes (putting the same jigsaw puzzle piece into the same spot over and over again trying to make it fit).

Learning from failure and redirecting leads to success, but you also must have a relentless mentality, which will help you weather the failures.

RELENTLESS MENTALITY

In *Relentless*, a book written by Michael Jordan's ex-trainer Tim S. Grover, the author explains why Michael Jordan was the best basketball player in the NBA. In short, it was because Michael Jordan was "relentless." Every time he hit a new goal (Most Valuable Player, world title, scoring champion, etc.), he made a new goal and continued to push himself to the limit in order to achieve it.

I, in no way, have the same athletic ability as Michael Jordan, but as I read that book, I couldn't help but think, "I think just like this guy, and that's why I have become so successful so quickly."

A relentless mentality means you are never satisfied. People with a relentless mentality have the mindset and the drive to be the best and to maintain that level of success. And when they reach their goal, it's not enough and they look for the next goal.

Pretend you have ten doors in front of you and you don't know what's on the other side of the doors. The only way to find out is to open a door and walk through it.

Approximately 70 percent of people look at the doors and don't open any. They're too scared because they don't know what's on the other side. They never find success. They'd rather sit in their misery knowing what to expect than dare to risk it all for something better. The book *Who Moved My Cheese?* discusses this problem in detail, and I suggest you read it after you finish this book.

Twenty percent open a door and when something bad happens, they give up, never opening another door. They never find success either. One bad day and they completely fall apart.

The remaining ten percent, those with a relentless mentality, open the doors until they find success. They understand that some doors may lead to negative results and they're willing to feel the pain. For example, when they walk through door number one and lose their money on a clueless business coach, they walk through door number two. When they walk through door number two and waste a bunch of money running Facebook ads improperly, they walk through door number three. When they walk through door number three and their girlfriends leave them because they are unsuccessful, they walk through door number four and get their first charge-back[2] from a customer they gave tons of attention to. Each time they make a choice and walk through the wrong door, something bad happens. But they learn from their mistakes (they don't go through the same door twice), and they don't give up, knowing that each time they open a door, it brings them closer to success. That's a relentless mentality.

I have a relentless mentality—I opened all ten doors—which is why my online business has become a success. During my first two years in business, I made only $2,000, my girlfriend broke up with me, my family told me I was an idiot, I was living in a 500-square-foot apartment, I drove a seventeen-year-old car, I worked a full-time job, and I made a ton of mistakes with my online business. Most people won't tolerate that and will quit. But I couldn't. I knew that if I kept trying, if I kept opening doors, working hard, and learning from my mistakes, that my business would succeed eventually. Now people pay me for advice in running their online businesses so they don't have to open all ten doors on their own. I know what's behind each

---

2   When a customer calls his credit card company and reports the charge as invalid or not authorized and you have to prove the charge was authorized. You'll eventually get the money back if your evidence is good enough, but it's a pain to deal with.

of those doors. Therefore, my clients only have to open the doors that lead to success.

Roadblocks are inevitable. When something doesn't work out, it leads you to another path of success—if you redefine success, learn from your failures, redirect, and have a relentless mentality.

I never imagined a career outside of the NFL, but when I tried to walk through that door, it slammed in my face. Instead of giving up and taking a job I didn't want, I worked hard and learned from my difficulties to create a highly successful online business. However, working hard and weathering difficulties were not enough to prevent me from failing along the way. They won't be enough for you either. You also need to be persistent, obtain the necessary tools that will enable you to become super successful, and work with a mentor who can guide you along the way.

CHAPTER 3

FAILING AND PERSISTENCE

Once football was no longer an option for me, I quit school—engineering wasn't for me, and I didn't want to work a nine-to-five job. But I wanted to make a high level of income. The only way to accomplish my goal was to start a business, but I didn't know how. A family friend, a well-known marketer who works from home and makes a multiple six-figure income (typically $200,000 or more), offered to mentor me, so I took the opportunity.

Over the next eight months, he taught me the process to create an online business and helped me build my first product, the Rapid Muscle System. Unfortunately, the strategies he taught me weren't the best strategies for a beginner, even though they were super beneficial to me down the road.

My product didn't sell well for three reasons:

1. I didn't have money to market the product.
2. I should have been selling the Rapid Muscle System for $2,000 or more instead of $47.
3. More people are interested in losing weight than in muscle building.

So it was the wrong strategy, the wrong offer, and the wrong product. However, since I was a beginner, I didn't know any better. That's why I believe it's vitally important to be coached by someone in *exactly* the position you wish to be in.

At that point, I was twenty-four years old, still living at home, working in my mentor's garage, and modeling to support myself. I decided I had to start living my life while continuing to make my online business work. After moving to Utah hoping to find a Latter-day Saints girl to get hitched to (I was fairly active at that time), I rented a small apartment and worked eight-hour shifts at Olive Garden six, sometimes seven, days a week. Between shifts, I'd work on my online business for another six to eight hours each day. Working sixteen hours a day left me with just enough time to go to the gym but no time for anything else.

After another long six months, my online business was still not making much money. I earned about $3,000 a month between Olive Garden and my business, with 99 percent of my income coming from Olive Garden, so I decided to quit Olive Garden and try door-to-door sales, believing I could make $150,000 in three months and then use that money to pay for ads to build my online business.

In my head, not being able to afford to purchase ads was the only thing holding me back. I see so many other business owners lie to themselves all the time with the "if I just had" belief. I honestly had many more issues than that, but again, I didn't know what I didn't know.

I moved to Alabama with my brother for the job, and we sold security alarms door-to-door. Door-to-door sales was the hardest thing I've ever done. I woke up at 5:00 a.m. to go to the gym before meeting the other salesmen at 8:00 a.m. We'd then typically drive two or two and a half hours to the towns where we were selling. After eating lunch in the car, I'd hit doors for seven or eight hours straight, until dark.

You're walking and the sun's beating down on you, people are cussing at you, calling the police on you, pulling a knife on you, or pointing a gun at you. And then you drive back home, arriving around 9:00 p.m., shower, go to bed, and do it all over again, six days a week. It sucks. On the weekends, I'd buy donuts with the guys and we'd just sit there and eat them, hoping for the summer to end sooner rather than later. That was our highlight, as bad as that sounds.

I made $50,000 to $60,000 or so over a five-month period, and even though I was one of the top rookie salesmen, I hated my life. Plus, I didn't make anything close to what I had been promised or hoped for. I felt desperate to find something better.

One day, I was scrolling through Facebook and saw an ad about how to build an online fitness business. I figured I had nothing to lose, so I clicked on the ad and then got on a phone call with someone. At that point, I had no idea what high-ticket sales were or what "high-ticket" meant, but he told me high-ticket sales were important for online business success.

Desperate to succeed and because I thought the program could help, I used the $2,000 I had left in my bank account for a down payment on the $5,000 program that promised to teach me the skills I needed. The additional $3,000 was charged to my credit card.

Turns out, I didn't know how to message potential buyers. If I had reached the right niche audience and followed through to make the sale, my first attempt to grow my muscle building and weight loss business may have worked. But I learned how to message potential buyers, walk them through a sales process, get them on a phone call, and close them (make the sale). Because I knew how to talk to people—I'd worked door-to-door sales and as a server—I was good at it. Compared to 90 percent of the other students, I was way ahead of the curve.

The program suggested I change my online business from muscle building to one-to-one fitness coaching and weight loss. I already had numerous personal training certifications, had been working out since I was twelve, and knew a lot about nutrition, so it was a good fit. I charged $2,000 for a four-month package, and in the first week, I made $10,000, triple what I was making at Olive Garden in a month. I also made more in a week than I made in a month while dripping with sweat and getting cussed out while working door-to-door sales.

I couldn't believe it was that easy.

I was so relieved and so excited, but I also felt like an idiot—I'd been so close the whole time. It felt like I'd wasted two years. If only someone had told me the right things to do early on, I would have hit my goal much faster than when I was on the wrong path.

I kept working the process and making more money. Then I ran ads to get more people to my page and used Instagram shout-outs[3] to get more people to follow me, find out their fitness goals, and engage them in a conversation, so

---

3   A shout-out is where you pay a bigger, more popular page to post your content with a call to action, typically to follow you.

I ultimately could get them to agree to a phone call where I would then sell them a training package.

It took me one year to make over $1 million.

In another three months, I'd made another $1 million.

Since then, I've made millions and millions and millions. In fact, at this moment, I make over $1.5 million in sales every single month and collect over $1 million of it up front.

But I wouldn't have done any of that if I hadn't persisted and figured out what worked for my online business.

A COACH'S ROLE IN BECOMING SUCCESSFUL

A coach gives you the tools you need to start your business. Think of it like writing this book. If I have an idea but don't know the process to write a book, my coach will help me figure out where to start (the table of contents) and tell me what to do once I've determined the content. It removes the guessing and keeps me focused.

Although my mentor taught me the wrong order of processes (processes that you must eventually learn to grow a big online business, but that are not necessary for a beginner to become successful), he led me down the right path.

Without his help, I wouldn't have known where to start. If you don't start, it's impossible to reach your goal.

It's important to ask for help and find a coach in your industry—someone who is successful at what you do. Most people don't want to ask for help for one of three reasons:

1. They don't want to admit they need help. Ego is the enemy here.
2. They don't think a coach will help. They're unwilling to admit they don't know it all.
3. They don't want to pay someone for help. They lie to themselves that one day they'll be able to afford it, which is the *exact* reason they need help *now*.

The number one reason people don't want to ask me for help is because they don't want to pay for a coach. They don't want to go into debt because they're too scared. They're not willing to take that risk. They also think that by trying to build a successful online business on their own, they're not wasting money, but in fact they are. It takes much longer to become successful if you don't factor in opportunity costs. For example, if you pay a coach $10,000 and he helps you make $30,000 in thirty days, you make a lot more money than the person who doesn't pay the coach and who only makes $30,000 a year. The person who doesn't pay the coach loses out on around $360,000 in potential revenue in a year (using the same theory of making $30,000 every 30 days) by deciding to hoard what little money he has.

Is a $10,000 investment on a credit card worth learning how to make $360,000 in a year and change your life forever? You tell me. Asking for help and going into debt is the only option if you're unhappy with your situation and want it to improve. I was more scared of being a loser than of being homeless. When you get to that point, when you feel frustrated, when you're killing yourself working twelve hours a day and only making a few thousand dollars for your efforts, when you're not hitting your goals, when you're tired of spinning your wheels and not going anywhere, you're willing to take a risk because you have no other choice.

You must be willing to experience inconvenience and sacrifice to make progress, and that means paying for a coach. You can spend $3,000 a month on rent for your apartment, or you can live with your parents and spend $3,000 a month on Facebook ads for your business. If you spend that money on ads, you're using it to grow your business. The same goes for coaches. If you spend money for a coach, you'll grow your business much faster and become successful at a higher level in a shorter period of time.

And success loves speed; most people need to win quickly or they'll quit, especially when they're working all the time and not finding financial success. The sooner you see some successes, the sooner your confidence will grow and you'll realize that this "online business thing" really works.

Money is a game. You must learn the game of money. If you're not making a lot, it means you don't understand the game. And those who do, those who are at the top of their field, will expect you to pay for their time. That's just how it works—to date I've spent over $500,000 on coaching. I will never ask someone to do anything more than I've done myself—that's a promise.

But always remember: Who you get your advice from is of the utmost importance. I personally wouldn't listen to Dave Ramsey on financial topics; his advice is geared toward people struggling to get out of credit card debt and not for people trying to become wealthy or leverage income like you.

The biggest risk an online business owner can take is not asking for help, which ultimately leads to not running the right way, and therefore losing time and money. That's time and money he can never get back.

But you need more than a good coach to succeed.

TOOLS TO BE SUPER SUCCESSFUL

When I began coaching people, I thought about what tools I wanted to share with them. I came up with three foundational tools that I—and most successful people—use.

LEARN HOW TO PROBLEM SOLVE ON YOUR OWN

I learned how to problem solve while working with my mentor. When I'd get stuck, I'd ask how to do something. In the beginning, he would help me, but after a few months, he became annoyed and told me to figure out the solutions on my own. (Much like my dad told me I had to get a job if I wanted to go to the movies.) When someone tells you what to do all the time, you become lazy. I realized he was right and knew I had to start figuring out things on my own. If I didn't, I'd be in trouble when he wasn't around to help me anymore. From that day forward, I started Googling everything. If I was using a certain software program and didn't understand how an aspect of it worked, I'd message support and ask. Problem solving on your own takes time—more time than getting a quick response from someone who already knows the answer—but you don't learn if you become lazy and let someone tell you what to do all the time. And you can't be a top business owner if you need other people to spell everything out for you. You must be able to problem solve.

Here are two examples:

1. During the coronavirus pandemic, every business had to deal with the consequences. Some business owners complained and did nothing. Others problem solved, adjusted what their business was doing (commercial meat distributors moving online and selling direct to consumers instead of direct to restaurants and other institutions), and made a ton of money.

2. My client Josh came to me when he was making approximately $15,000 per month. He'd already worked with three coaches; all told him to run a webinar, a fairly common marketing strategy, if he wanted to make more money. He did it, but the webinar didn't translate into additional sales, and he was frustrated. I signed him up for my coaching services, and within four days he wanted to quit and asked for a refund. After convincing him to stick with me and to change his business approach, he made over $100,000 per month within three months. When he asked questions, instead of spoon-feeding him the answers, I broke down the problem and asked questions that would lead him to the answer. I also encouraged him to try new approaches, look at the resulting data, and problem solve. For example, if Josh said he wasn't getting enough leads, I'd ask how much money he was spending. If the answer was $1,000, I'd say, "If a lead costs $10 and you are not getting enough leads, then why don't you spend more money?" Once Josh saw positive results, he gained confidence. Now he's able to problem solve on his own. If I

hadn't helped him and he hadn't gained confidence, he never would have believed he could solve problems on his own, an important skill he needs to run a successful business.

UNDERSTAND THAT ALL YOUR HARD WORK WILL GIVE YOU THE SKILLS YOU NEED TO BECOME SUCCESSFUL

Each job requires a particular skillset. It could be how to talk to others, how to make sales, how to perform consistently, how to remain dedicated to your work, etc. These skills are the backbones of success. My door-to-door sales work taught me how to sell, including reading body language, fighting objections, and being quick on my feet. That skill translated into my online business. Remember Bo, the investment firm salesman I told you about earlier who sold mutual funds and other products to financial advisors? His sales background and his ability to talk to others gave him the skills he needed to transition much easier into running a successful online business. Same with Tikis and Amanda. Their ability to successfully interact with others, combined with their hard work and dedication to their nine-to-five jobs, gave them the perseverance and diligence they needed to make their online fitness business a success.

IF YOU FAIL, GET BACK UP AND DO WHAT IS NECESSARY TO BECOME SUCCESSFUL, EVEN WHEN YOU DON'T FEEL LIKE IT

Quitting when you fail is not an option if you want to become successful. Believe me, I know. I almost quit many times when starting my online business. Every time I got to that point, I'd call my mentor and he'd talk me out of it, insisting I'd figure out what to do in order to become a success. He always pointed out that I was smart, that I had a good work ethic, and that he was there to support me no matter what.

You must keep going even when you fail. You must keep opening doors. If you quit, you get nothing. You have no chance to succeed. You must deal with adversity and keep working hard. Why do so many rich kids fail in the business world? Because they've had everything handed to them; they became entitled. They didn't have to work hard, to deal with adversity, to fail and get back up again, to fight for what they want. After dealing with adversity my entire life, encountering adversity in the business world was expected and not difficult to deal with for the most part. I'd already dealt with so much hardship that anything I encountered when building my business seemed easy in comparison.

There's an image on the internet of two guys digging for gold down a tunnel (if you search for "guy digging for gold," you will see it). The first guy stops an inch before he reaches the gold and walks back in defeat. The second guy digs his way through and finds the gold. That image illustrates how people give up too soon. They either don't work long enough at something or stop after a failure, quitting right before they find success. I could have quit too soon, but thanks to my mentor who kept encouraging me (and a lot of grit on my part), I didn't.

If you look at famous people who achieved success—Oprah Winfrey, Jennifer Lopez, Barack Obama, Donald Trump, Elon Musk, Mark Zuckerberg, Jeff Bezos, Mark Cuban—they've all navigated failures along the way. It's inevitable. If you want to build a civilization on the moon, do you really think you will figure out how to do it correctly the first time? No. If you go into something knowing you will experience failure, it's easier to tolerate when failure occurs. And if you happen to get lucky and achieve success on the first try, that's an anomaly, but a good one.

Failure is part of success. It's not just a nice saying—it's true. What's important is that you have the resiliency to keep going. That's what sets apart those who succeed from those who don't.

Find that one person who has your back, who you go to for encouragement when you're struggling. His or her support will keep you going—even when you want to quit.

As you can see, a mentor helps by providing you with the tools you need to become successful. You will fail along the way, but it's important to get back up and try and try again until you achieve success.

In addition to the personal tools for success, you also must possess practical tools to build your business and know how to implement them.

PART 2

PRACTICAL ADVICE TO BUILD YOUR BUSINESS

CHAPTER 4

WILL YOUR BUSINESS
WORK ONLINE?

Before I started my online business, I talked to trainers at the gym where I worked out because I was thinking about becoming a personal trainer. I loved fitness, so it seemed like a logical choice. The trainers were killing themselves, training ten to twelve clients per day, an hour per client. Some clients were whiners; others wouldn't show up for their appointments.

When I found out how much the trainers were making, that they had to give a bunch of the money they earned to the gym, and that there was a cap on their income because the only way to make more money was to take on more clients, I knew training in a gym wasn't right for me. Once a trainer runs out of hours in the week or runs out of available clients, he can't make additional money. Plus, it's tiring to talk to people all day long unless you love it.

It was essential for me to work at something I love and to have an unlimited income. The only way for me to accomplish that goal was to create an online business, providing clients with the same workouts, only not in person. If I could send a client his workouts and his meal plan, and text him what to do, the client would not need an in-person trainer.

Most of my clients don't care how they reach their goals; they just want results. I provide a weekly workout plan and ask the clients if it looks okay. Ninety percent of the time, they like it. If not, I customize the plan based on the client's concerns. Each client's video workout program uses similar exercises, because there are only so many exercises you can do to target specific muscle groups. However, if a client has a special need or condition, I'll customize the videos for him. The app I use provides access to an exercise database and enables me to change exercises within the workout as a client progresses. I use a similar app for nutrition programs, inputting the client's personal food choices along with the required daily calories. The app generates a meal plan, which I then send to the client. If the client doesn't like the meal plan, I change it.

People think it matters a lot which exercises you do and what you eat, but it really doesn't. If someone works out fifteen minutes every day for the rest of his life, he'll look way better than someone who works out twelve hours a day for three months. It's consistency that matters. As long as my clients enjoy the program, they will continue to follow it. If they don't enjoy it, it's easy for me to quickly make changes so that they do.

The beauty of all this is that instead of getting paid for my time, I'm now being paid for my results. That's what great about online business. When done right, you will be paid for a specific result instead of your time, and that's how you can create massive income.

Online is the perfect platform for fitness and other businesses. But before deciding if your business will succeed online, ask yourself a few questions.

IS IT NECESSARY TO SEE YOUR CLIENT IN PERSON?

Moving your business online gives you the potential to blow it up exponentially. With an in-person business, you're limited in the number of clients you can work with on a daily, weekly, and monthly basis. Online, there is no limit; you can reach as many people as you want, especially once you start growing a team of employees. I went from seeing seven or eight clients per day to being able to handle thirty at a time myself. Once I starting hiring coaches to help me, we were able to handle hundreds. And instead of having to buy my own gym to expand my income, I only needed enough clients to justify hiring another trainer to coach them. That's how I scaled my business. It's how you can too—every time you get too many clients, hire another trainer (for a fitness-based business) or coach (for other types of businesses). This process enables your company to keep growing infinitely.

The question to ask yourself is: Do I need to see my clients in person to get results?

Unless you're a doctor, a chiropractor, a dentist, or someone who has to touch the person's body to perform your services, the answer is no.

Keep in mind, while I'm using personal training as an example, moving online can work for a plethora of other businesses including real estate investing (teaching others how to make real estate deals), advertising copywriting (teaching how to write copy), ad agencies (teaching clients how to run ads), mindset coaching, lifestyle coaching, and Amazon store creators (how to create a store for another business and sell products). For additional examples, go to https://www.infiniteincomebook.com/course-ideas.

CAN YOU LEVERAGE YOUR TIME?

If you're a trainer at a gym, you can't leverage your time.

You always have to work at the gym. Same for a dentist—he can't clean people's teeth over the internet.

In order to leverage your time, you must be able to hire someone to coach your clients online. For example, can I hire someone to teach people online how to do a handstand? Yes. Can I hire someone to teach people online how to work out? Yes.

I rarely coach anymore. My team coaches my clients. If I worked by myself, I could only coach a specific number of people each day and would have no time to scale my business. However, if I hire additional coaches to work with the clients, I have the necessary time. Clients are happy working with my coaches. They don't expect me, the company's CEO, to work with them, just like they wouldn't expect the CEO of Apple or IBM to work with them. Plus, if it were possible to work with the CEO, it might cost three times as much (or more) for the same result as working with a member of his team. Why would someone want to pay that when he can get the same service for less?

But if someone is willing to pay much more for the personal attention of the CEO and if the CEO is willing and available to coach him, that's great too.

You need to consider two things if you want to start an online business:

1. Can you use video to provide your offer?
2. Can you hire others down the road to provide the services once you step back to focus on scaling your business?

Keep in mind that the material you provide to clients will be uploaded to a membership site in the form of a video.

WHAT ARE THE DIFFERENCES FOR YOUR BUSINESS BETWEEN ONLINE AND IN-PERSON SERVICES?

Selling online is all about figuring out what the market wants and using it to your advantage. If someone asks me why she should pay for an online trainer when she can get someone to work with her in person, I inform her that the in-person trainer doesn't want her to learn how to do the exercises on her own. The trainer wants her to keep paying for the trainer's services forever. I, on the other hand, because I run my business online, teach my clients how to do the exercises on their own. That's marketing; that's sales. You give people what they want (an exercise program) and you say it in a way that convinces them you have the answer (I'll teach you how to do the exercises so you won't have to pay forever).

If you're a physical therapist, can you switch your offer from providing in-person services to providing an online program? For example, what if you sold a course that showed people stretches and exercises to strengthen their back?

VIDEOS FOR SERVICE OFFERS

The videos are created by recording video calls with clients where you teach the clients what you are offering (exercises, how to clean your teeth, etc.). Whenever you create new material, you create a new video and add the video to the membership site. Eventually, you'll have created a video to cover each aspect of your offer, eliminating the need to create additional videos.

Video is great, because if one client has a question about what you are teaching, chances are another will. While creating the video, you have the opportunity to address those questions as they occur. You also can edit the video, if you desire, before uploading it to the membership site.

Don't worry if the video doesn't look perfect. Clients simply want results; they won't care how pretty your video looks if what you teach doesn't work. As your business grows, you can go back and make things "nicer" if you wish.

If a client gets stuck or doesn't understand something, he will contact you. This is when you take the relationship offline and message the client over Facebook or talk to the client on a Zoom call to clarify. You personally engage in this process until you earn enough money to pay someone else to do it for you.

If you only provide one-to-one coaching, you overtax your coaches—they're doing the same thing over and over again with each client. But if clients watch videos online and contact the coaches only when they don't understand something, it frees up the coaches' time to be able to handle many clients instead of only a few, which in turn helps the business grow.

How about financial advisors? They always have to sit down and be right in front of a client, right? No—they can also record financial instruction videos and sell the videos online. Obviously, some one-to-one attention will still be involved, especially when charging a lot of money, but I hope you see the point.

A dentist can't clean teeth online, but he can focus on a particular aspect of his business and sell that online. For example, the dentist could show clients how to keep their teeth clean at home (at a level similar to the quality of cleaning they would receive at the dentist's office), so they only have to see the dentist for a cleaning once every three years instead of once a year. People will buy that.

Almost any business can be translated to an online business if you figure out your niche and what you have to offer.

In order to ensure your offer generates a high income, you need to consider several factors.

IS YOUR OFFER BROAD ENOUGH TO REACH A LARGE ONLINE AUDIENCE?

The easiest way to determine if your offer is broad enough is to determine if you can run Facebook ads for the offer that target a large online audience. While there are many platforms you can run ads on (YouTube and Google being the two other prominent ones), Facebook is the most used and the easiest for a beginner to navigate. It is also the cheapest in terms of ad cost.

Facebook determines who will see your ad based on the parameters you set for the ad, so you want to be able to reach as many viewers as possible.

Here are three examples. The first two show offers that are scalable; the third does not. Compare them and see how they differ.

1. Basketball: If you're selling something related to basketball, you want Facebook to show the ad to anyone who has ever interacted with basketball pages, posted about basketball, played basketball, etc. However, not every person who sees your ad will want your offer. Some might not even like basketball; they may have accidentally clicked "like" on a basketball-related page or stopped playing basketball when they were eight years old. However, this offer is still scalable because there are many people who play and/or like basketball.

2. Amazon: If you want to teach others how to make money on Amazon (as opposed to making money on Amazon with a specific item), that's a scalable offer. You can run Facebook ads to anyone who likes Amazon, online business, making money, etc.

3. Book writing: If you want to help eighth graders write

books and you run a Facebook ad, only eighth graders will see your ad and can buy your offer. Some eighth graders may hate writing; some may not want help; some may not have money of their own to spend; and there's just not a whole lot of eighth graders in general. This offer is not scalable because it's too limited.

If an offer is super specific, it's a bad offer because it can't be scaled. You only have so much control over who sees your ad on Facebook. It's best to look toward offering something that can reach a larger audience. Coaching (or consulting of any kind) is an area that can easily reach a large online audience (and what I'm a huge proponent of). So are video courses showing how to build an amazing garden, how to lose weight, how to lower stress, how to do yoga, etc. Each of these topics is wide enough to include a majority of people who might be interested in the offer. If the offer is how to run backward on a treadmill, not too many people will be interested in that, so the audience size becomes too narrow.

Coaches often niche down too much. That's a mistake. If you will only work with moms who have three kids, for example, you're excluding moms who have more or fewer than three kids. It's too narrow. But if you want to work with busy moms so they don't go crazy from dealing with their kids, you will have a much larger online audience. Niching down is powerful because it draws in people who feel your offer is right for them. But if you niche down too much, you repel a lot of people who would have become clients.

Don't get it twisted. I'm not saying niching down is bad; I'm saying not to do it too much. Remember the story of Goldilocks and the Three Bears? Remember when she eats all three bowls of porridge? One is too hot, one is too cold, and the other is just right? It's the same with narrowing down a niche—you have to find the spot that's just right.

CAN YOU SELL YOUR BUSINESS OFFER AT A PREMIUM PRICE?

A premium price, on average, is $3,000 for a three- to four-month period of services. In order to charge a premium price, it's important to offer something that is tangible, measurable, and has specific results.

Almost everything people want—getting fit, better health, making money, improved relationships, learning a new skill or hobby, etc.—falls into one of three categories:

1. Health: how to lose weight, how to sleep better, how to have less stress or anxiety.
2. Wealth: how to invest, how to build a business, how to run social media ads, how to grow a social media following.
3. Relationships: how to navigate an open relationship,

how to save your marriage from divorce, how to pick up a girl you are interested in dating.

Determine if your offer falls within one of the categories. If your offer doesn't fall into one of the categories (for example, how to play video games better), you won't be able to sell it at a premium price. Playing video games better doesn't make someone healthier, doesn't make someone wealthier, and it doesn't improve relationships. Are there some people who would buy that product? Sure, but there are not a lot.

Most people want to make more money. Most want to be healthier. And most also want better relationships. They are willing to pay a premium price to get those things, but only if they see tangible results, such as losing thirty pounds in four months or making $100,000 in six months. That's a high level of service with a specific result, one that justifies charging a premium price.

As you can see, most businesses don't need a physical presence. Unless you're a doctor who needs to see a patient with cancer, a dentist who needs to clean teeth, or a plumber who needs to fix a toilet, virtually any business can go online. Even the plumber can move part of his business online by asking, "Can I create a video to sell to clients that would enable them to copy my actions to fix a specific problem on their own and obtain the same results without me physically being present?" Ninety-nine percent of the time, the answer is yes.

I went from what is traditionally an in-person, face-to-face business to an online business and became more successful than I ever could have imagined.

You can too.

However, you must know the do's and don'ts in building an online business if you want to be successful.

CHAPTER 5

THE DO'S AND DON'TS IN BUILDING AN ONLINE BUSINESS

To date, I've spent approximately $540,000 on business coaches. That's a lot of money in three years. My first coach cost $5,000, which I paid for with my savings and a credit card. He showed me the basics. Once I made enough money, I hired another coach to show me the next steps—he cost somewhere between $10,000 and $15,000 and recommended I build and offer many products, even though I was a one-man team. That didn't make much sense, so I fired him and hired a third coach to learn how to run ads so I could reach more people with my offer. He also cost $10,000. Instead of teaching me how to run ads, he taught me how to run a webinar, hoping it would work to jump-start my business, which it didn't. Moving on to my fourth coach didn't help either. Neither did my fifth.

I was killing myself to make the money to pay these coaches, and they were terrible. I was depressed, working a crazy number of hours, and feeling frustrated, knowing I could have saved the money I'd spent on coaches and used it for something else instead of throwing it away.

However, after hiring my fifth coach, I figured out conversion conversations (which I'll show you how to use in chapter 6), and my business took off. How? From trial and error. Unless you can't learn from your failures, you're bound to figure out the missing pieces eventually, right?

I went from making $30,000 to $50,000 in a month to making $30,000 to $50,000 in a week, and it grew from there. Since then, I've paid coaches whenever I set new goals, need new systems, or need help with technology. But I've gotten far better at choosing coaches who can truly help me.

Why the coaches I chose weren't right for me:

1. They Used Group Coaching: In group coaching, most of the answers to questions are general rather than specific. For example, if attempt A doesn't work, try attempt B. It's the same answer for all those who are

being coached. This process was very frustrating for me. I needed a coach who would look at what I was doing and provide situation-specific suggestions.

2. The Coaches' Process Didn't Work for What I Was Seeking: Every coach I hired was only making a couple hundred thousand dollars more than me, and they'd been in the game for four or five years longer (some dozens of years longer). I would easily and quickly catch up to them in terms of total sales if I knew what to do. Their processes didn't work to scale their businesses up to a high level.

What I don't like about the coaching industry—and what I wanted to change when I got into it—is that people would go through a program, and if it didn't work, the coach would state the failure was the client's fault. Clients, on the other hand, would state that it was the coach's fault and that the program failed them.

In my biased opinion, if you go through my program and can't make money online, you're not going to go through anyone else's program and make money because very few have scaled their business as fast as me. No other coach I know of is making $1.5 million-plus per month and also providing one-to-one coaching (in addition to the video content) to all their clients. That's a lot of work. But one-to-one coaching is what's effective. It's personalized to your specific situation. You'll learn from my mistakes. It's what you need if you want to become successful.

MY SIX BIGGEST MISTAKES

My first four mistakes are related to my personal coaching, while the remaining two relate to clients and employees.

1. **Waiting Too Long to Hire a Coach:** For two long years, while struggling to make money with my online business, I kept telling myself I couldn't afford to hire a business coach. Nothing I was doing was working, and I was frustrated. Finally, desperate and determined to make my business a success, I decided I'd do whatever it took to pay for business coaching rather than fail—max out my credit cards, take out loans, become homeless, etc. I finally hired a business coach, who I should have hired a lot sooner. When you hire a coach—even if it's not the right one or if the coach gives you bad advice—you learn what not to do in your business, and that helps you learn what to do in order to become successful. Sure, that's an expensive way to learn, but you're sacrificing money for speed, so you succeed much faster. If you really want to be rich, a multimillionaire or a billionaire, is $10,000 for a coach really a lot of money? No, it's not if you're making a lot of money. But it is a lot when you don't make a lot, so it feels out of reach. However, you can't make a lot of money if you don't know how to make it. That's where the experts come in—the coaches. You need to take that financial risk and take it early so you don't struggle for years like I did.

2. **Hiring People Who Have Never Done What I**

Wanted to Do: You don't hire someone who plays soccer to teach you to play baseball. And you don't hire a business coach who has never worked out and knows nothing about the fitness industry to teach you how to create a massive fitness business. Unfortunately, that's what I did. The coaches I hired assumed that selling fitness packages would be the same as selling business packages, but they're not. Therefore, the advice the coaches gave me wasn't working, and I wasn't making the sales I needed to create a successful business.

3. **Not Trusting My Gut:** I hired five different coaches. I knew that what they were telling me to do was stupid and that it wouldn't work. But I didn't trust my gut to go in a different direction. If I had, it would have saved me time and money. And had I hired them early on in the process (as I explained in point number one), I would have figured that out sooner, making my business a success much quicker.

4. **Following a Coach Word for Word:** When you hire a coach, it's common to do everything he tells you, even if you know something isn't working for your business. Following the coach word for word slows down your progress. In addition, if you listen to a coach too closely, you stop thinking for yourself and become reliant on the coach for everything. This prevents you from learning to solve your own problems. Ultimately, I learned to listen to what my coach told me and took

that and adapted it to fit my business in my unique style, which worked better and helped my business grow faster.

5. **Not Understanding How Much People Need to Be Spoon-Fed:** People need new information and processes broken down into simple steps, or they will not understand what to do. Just because it's easy for me to do something (an exercise or a sales call, for example), it doesn't mean it's easy for my client to learn how to do it. So if you're teaching someone how to make a peanut butter sandwich, you need to tell him in steps:

   - Step One: Open the bread bag.
   - Step Two: Grab a piece of bread.
   - Step Three: Get a knife.
   - Step Four: Open the peanut butter.
   - Step Five: Spread the peanut butter onto the bread, etc.

   By breaking information and processes down into simplistic steps, people understand what you are trying to convey and don't get lost.

6. **Not Knowing How to Teach People:** When I first started my online business, I thought all I needed to do was show someone something one time and then they were ready to do it on their own. But that doesn't work. People don't learn that quickly. The best way to teach others is to engage in the process with them:

- Have your client watch you doing what you are trying to teach.
- Repeat the last step several times.
- Have the client perform the task or exercise while you watch.
- Provide feedback to your client so he can improve the process.
- Once the client understands the process and can do it on his own, let him run with it.

DO'S AND DON'TS

I subscribe to the "fail fast and learn" school of thought. By reviewing my mistakes, I was able to determine the things you should and shouldn't do to start and run your online business. I'm saving you a lot of time, money, and frustration with these lists.

DON'T:

- Hire Someone in the Business-to-Business Space When Your Offer Is in the Business-to-Consumer Space, or Vice Versa: The mistake I made was never hiring someone who had built a successful online fitness business when I was creating my first online business. I kept hiring coaches who provided business coaching to teach me how to build a fitness business. The business-to-business space is very different than the business-to-consumer space. Fortunately, I've built a seven-figure business in each sector so I understand the nuances.

- Focus on Unnecessary Things: At the end of the day, the only thing that matters in business is making money. People waste a lot of time designing their logos, designing email headers, creating websites, etc. However, potential clients don't care about logos, email headers, and websites. Focus instead on activities that help generate money—it's that plain and simple. I began selling training packages without a website, without sending emails, without a calendar link, etc. I reached out to people via social media to book phone calls and sold them that way. All they cared about was if I could help them get results. Spend your time making your first $10,000, because that first $10,000 will enable your business to grow much faster than making a nice website with money you don't have.

- Rely on One Method of Traffic: Relying on one method of traffic is dangerous as you grow your business. You may have only one source of traffic in the beginning stages, but what if something happens and one day your entire business is gone? For example, if Facebook decides it doesn't like my business and shuts down my account, and if that's the only place that drives traffic to my business, I'm in trouble. Now I can't pay my team and I can't make money. But if I'm on Google, YouTube, LinkedIn, Facebook, and Instagram, my business would survive if one or more platforms deleted my business account. Therefore, it's important to diversify as quickly as possible.

- Start with a Low-Ticket Offer: A low-ticket offer is difficult to refine and make work. If you don't have money and you're selling something—a book, for example—for $47, you need to sell one million books or more for it to change your life. If you don't have money, how are you going to pay for ads to sell that many copies? Even if you sold only 1,000 copies without having to rely on ads, you would make $47,000 before the cost of doing business. However, if your profit margin is 10 percent, meaning it costs you 90 percent of the purchase price to sell that book, you end up with only $4,700 for your efforts. Low-ticket offers are usually reserved for experienced marketers or companies that make millions of dollars and can afford to go into the red (lose money) for three months. Now that my business is successful, I use low-ticket offers. I know that I'll make up the 50 percent loss in income in ninety days because the low-ticket offer will provide leads to whom I can then sell high-ticket offers. The goal is to sell high-ticket offers, meaning an item or service that costs a lot of money—it's how you make money faster.

- Blame Others for Your Failures: When I first hired my coaches, I did everything they told me to do until I'd exhausted my options. At first, when I wasn't achieving the success I wanted, I thought I was doing something wrong and asked myself what I could do better. What part of the coach's strategy was I not executing properly? Instead of blaming someone else for my inability to make my business a success, I exhausted my resources and options and pushed myself to my limit, until I found the techniques and skills I needed to achieve success. Most people don't put in the necessary time and effort. They don't push hard to succeed and then assume the advice they were given was wrong. They blame others for their failures.

DO:

- Pick Something You Know Will Make Money: If you want your online business to be successful, you must sell something that you know will make money and that also matches your skillset. (Revisit the previous chapter to make an informed choice.) Once you have money, you can follow your passion. The saying "Follow your passion and you'll never work a day in your life" is relative. It depends on your goal. If your goal is to be happy and to follow your dreams, not caring if you make money along the way, then follow your passion. However, if your goal is to retire young and to have a lot of money, you need to follow what you're good at, not your passion. I'm a big fan of going all in on something, but I'm also a fan of being realistic about your abilities. I can sing all day long, but I'll never become a professional singer—that's not my skillset. But I'm really good at fitness and business coaching, and I know how to help people make a lot of money. And now that I have money, I have the time and the financial means to follow my passion for traveling, hunting, etc.

- Hire a Coach Who Is Financially Where You Want to Be: It's important to hire someone who can help you reach the level of success you desire because he's done it himself. Before I began coaching others on how to build their online businesses, I grew my online business to a $1 million-plus-per-year business.

- Hire the Right People: As your business grows, it's important to hire people who can replace you and do the job well. As I stated earlier, the goal is to free up your time from taking sales calls, closing deals, and coaching people so you can focus on the higher-level aspects of your business, such as developing new products, marketing, etc. Once your company starts to make a lot of money, there's no longer time for you to do everything on your own anymore. And if you have to work all the time, it defeats the purpose of making a lot of money. Therefore, your business is only as good as your team. If you hire people who are lazy or don't do their jobs well, your business won't do well. You must hire people who are knowledgeable, dedicated, hardworking, and have a non-entitlement attitude—people you can trust so you don't have to work all the time anymore.

- Give One-to-One Coaching Specific to Needs and Problems: If I sent you a course on how to fix a car engine and you didn't understand something, what would you do? You would be stuck, right? But if I also provided one-on-one coaching, you could contact me for clarification, next steps, and encouragement. One-on-one coaching costs more because it requires additional time and prevents the coach from working on other aspects of the business that generate money. But it's more effective. Rather than feeling frustrated and giving up, clients move faster toward their goals. Immediately solving problems also provides positive reinforcement and encourages clients to continue along their path instead of giving up.

- Move Fast: Many people are really slow. For example, a guy might read a book about how to fix a car engine but doesn't do anything with it. Information works only if you implement it. As soon as you are told to implement specific processes in your online business, you should start doing so immediately. There is no other way to get results. If you just nod your head and do nothing else, or if you take forever to implement something, your business will not succeed.

You don't have to spend $540,000 like I did to learn how to run an online business and make it a success. But it is important to understand conversion conversations if you want your business to blow up in a good way.

CHAPTER 6

THE SECRET METHOD THAT BLEW UP MY BUSINESS IN A GOOD WAY

Every coach I hired told me to use the same method to get sales: run ads on Facebook, sit back, and hope it leads prospective clients to book sales calls with me. But it didn't work. The coaches would insist my video that ran with the ad was ineffective, so I'd change it and then change it again. I kept changing things, and nothing worked. I tried eight hundred different angles. I was angry and frustrated to the point of desperation, but still determined to make my business a success.

Not knowing what else to do and willing to try anything, I decided to message people who came into my Facebook

Messenger via an ad. When running ads on Facebook, you have two options:

1. You can have them click an ad and go straight to a web page.
2. You can have them click an ad that will then open up in Facebook Messenger (and you can send them to a page from there).

At the time, I didn't know that the simple tweak of messaging people who came into my Facebook Messenger from an ad would explode my business, but it made all the difference. I'd never done that before, as dumb as it sounds. And none of my coaches had told me to do it either. Within a few hours, I made seven sales phone calls and closed six of them, earning myself a quick $20,000. I thought: Holy shit! I figured it out, all because of those ads.

Keep in mind that just sending people to Facebook Messenger isn't enough to blow up your business. The follow-up I used was the key, but until that point, I had been sold on the dream of 100 percent automation—and that was why I had been losing for so long.

Once I knew what worked, I realized it didn't matter if prospective clients watched my video sales letter.[4] What mattered was that I direct messaged them and convinced

---

4   A video where I explain my offer and service.

them to get on a sales phone call with me, where ultimately I could make the sale. It was a surefire path that I knew would work over and over again.

Once you get ads to work and understand how to follow up with prospective clients, you can make someone (who has no idea who you are) buy something from you. That's how you have unlimited potential.

If you follow my process and method, which I call *conversion conversations*, it will blow up your sales. Conversion conversations connect you with potential buyers via direct message on social media (Facebook, Instagram, LinkedIn, etc.), and those messages ultimately lead to a phone call, which then leads to a sale.

Ninety-nine percent of you probably think you already do this and do it well when in reality you either don't do it or do a terrible job. Some tell me, "Oh yeah, that's so easy. I already do that," to which I politely respond, "Then why aren't you making over $1 million a month?"

Conversion conversations are a method that works and a skill that can be learned.

WHY CONVERSION CONVERSATIONS ARE IMPORTANT

Conversion conversations create a one-to-one relationship. For example, if you're in the market for a house and a realtor calls you ten times while every other realtor calls you only once and sends you an email about the house for sale, who are you more likely to buy the house from? The person who called you ten times or the person who called you once? You will buy from the person who called you ten times, because sales are relationship-based, and they're trust-based. Putting forth a one-to-one effort and speaking with potential customers always leads to more sales compared to sending an email or running an ad and not following up to create a one-to-one relationship. No matter how good a marketer's automation is, he will never beat one-to-one personal touch. You can be lazy, automate everything, and struggle endlessly. Or you can add in personal touch, which is more difficult, but you'll beat *all* the competition.

Do conversion conversations require more effort? Sure. But they also lead to a lot of sales. If you automate your business, hoping people will simply sign up to purchase your services, you're losing opportunities to make sales, especially when people like me and my team are messaging those clients. Unlike you, I'm creating trust in both me and my product, so by the time I talk to potential clients on the phone, they're ready to buy.

Conversion conversations will increase your sales rate tremendously. Once I began using them, my closing percentage (the percentage of people I went through an hour call with and sold) went from 30 percent to 70 percent.

HOW TO INCREASE YOUR CONVERSION RATE BY UP TO 50 PERCENT

The conversion conversation process enables my company to maintain contact with prospective clients. Even if a prospective client clicks on an ad that takes her to a video and then she clicks off, she receives a direct message from me (or my team) thirty minutes later—that's what sets my business apart from the millions of other businesses that run ads. The direct message says something like this: "Hey, Janice. What's up? So you clicked on the ad. How did you like the video? What questions do you have?" It's not some automated BS the prospect can smell from a mile away.

This direct message reengages Janice, and now she remembers me and we're having a conversation. The conversation leads her to book a phone call with me that she wouldn't have booked if I hadn't direct messaged her. Direct messaging increases the conversion rate tremendously. It draws people who initially were too busy, didn't understand, didn't like your video, didn't like your page, etc., back into the process to become a buyer.

It allows the average marketer (like me) to beat the best of the best with ease. Think about it. I've owned a business for three years and done over $20 million in sales at the time I'm writing this. How many people do you know that have grown that fast with zero help or funding?

Imagine Company A obtains a thousand leads per day but doesn't message anyone. Maybe it sends potential customers emails and videos, hoping to make a sale. Company B messages every potential customer. Which company is going to make more sales? Company B—the company that uses a more personal touch. Responding with a personal touch shows you care. I've tested this process and it works. And whenever I see something that works, I double down.

Many of you will feel this process is too much work, so you won't do it, but then you'll wonder why you didn't hit your financial goals.

Stop trying to find the path of least resistance and just do what works.

PERSONAL TOUCH WILL ALWAYS BEAT AUTOMATION

I can sell someone all day long if I can talk to him.

What's hard is selling to people you can't talk to as a result of automating everything.

It's easier to convince a potential client to take action if you personally reach out to the client instead of waiting for him to click on ads and videos, hoping he'll buy what you're selling. Most salespeople are unsuccessful when using advertising because they don't reach out to potential clients, which requires additional effort. Trying to automate everything requires so much more testing, money, and wasted time. I prefer efficiency.

In life, anything that takes more effort—working out at the gym, relationships, saving money, etc.—typically works out in your favor only if you put forth the necessary effort. Business is the same. If I put more effort into reaching out to potential clients, I make more money. It works. And more importantly, it takes the pressure off my marketing. If my marketing is ineffective, it doesn't matter. I'm going to message clients to make personal connections and sell them my products. If I don't message clients, my company's marketing must be the best in the world in order to successfully compete in the marketplace. Remember, when starting an online business, you most likely won't have the skillset to compete with established marketers who have been in the business for twenty years. Personal touch allows you to get away with more. You don't have to be as skilled at marketing, as long as you put forth the effort and personally reach out to potential clients.

That's why personal touch beats automation.

CONTROLLING YOUR BUSINESS WITH CONVERSION CONVERSATIONS

The process of conversion conversations allows you to control your business. It provides opportunity to make mistakes without suffering consequences. If your video ad stinks, it doesn't matter, because you always message potential clients and convince them to talk to you on the phone. If your emails aren't read by potential clients, it doesn't matter, because you always message potential clients and convince them to talk to you on the phone.

If your business doesn't use conversion conversations, you are crossing your fingers and leaving success up to chance, hoping potential clients click through and sign up for sales calls. Utilizing conversion conversations gives your business predictability. It gives it consistency. And it gives you peace of mind month after month after month. Your business will beat the competitor every time.

Don't rely on chance by setting up your business, leaving it, and hoping it works. What works are conversion conversations.

However, conversion conversations are only one tool in your business toolbox. You also need to know the correct way to engage in phone sales if you want to be successful.

CHAPTER 7

PHONE SALES

Phone sales play an important part in making a lot of sales and scaling your business, because talking to potential clients on the phone is the easiest, most effective way to build trust. And trust is the cornerstone of a long, fruitful business relationship with your client.

When you hear someone's voice, his tone, and his inflection, it helps you respond appropriately. When he hears your voice, your tone, your inflection, and how you are treating him, he develops trust—it's the nature of talking to someone. The more you talk, the more you build trust. Here's an example of what I mean: If you have a disagreement with a friend via text messaging, it's hard to win. The voice, tone, and inflection are lost. As a result, the disagreement can potentially continue forever. However, if you have an in-person disagreement with a friend and she can hear your voice, your tone, and your inflection, it's easier to respond appropriately, and the disagreement will end in a timelier manner.

Trust isn't the only positive side effect of phone sales, however. If I'm on the phone with a potential client who has agreed to take the call, it's the equivalent of me standing in front of him. It's hard to hang up and hard to get rid of me because most people inherently don't want to be rude. If the only way to get out of a situation is to be rude or to lie, most people won't do it. It's much easier to ignore someone via email or text than it is on a phone call. Obviously, some people won't buy what you're selling, and you'll reach the end of the call having wasted your time. But you have a much greater chance of making that sale because you come face-to-face with potential clients. Phone sales give you greater control over the outcome, simply because the only way to leave the call is to hang up.

Phone sales also give potential clients the opportunity to ask specific questions and obtain fast responses, which also contributes to establishing trust.

For example, if a potential client asks, "What makes you different than the rest of the coaches?"

I'll say, "I built a seven-figure business-to-consumer business and a seven-figure business-to-business company.

Most of these other coaches only business coach. Who do you think is more qualified? Someone who built a business before teaching, or someone who started teaching without ever having built a business?"

If a potential client asks, "Do you just run webinars?"

I'll say, "No, that's not enough to be successful. It's all in the follow-up. That's why I teach my clients conversion conversations, and if you sign up, that's the bulk of our training."

If a potential client lands on a sales page and doesn't understand it or doesn't agree with it, he clicks off and goes on with his life. If you convince that same person to take a free phone call with you, you can turn that non-sale into a sale.

Developing personal relationships via phone sales enables you to charge more money. People are more willing to spend more for your services or products when they trust you.

Phone sales are the easiest way to get results. They don't require a high amount of skill (as much skill as automation). They're an important tool in your toolbox.

Before I show you how to structure the phone call and what to say, let's discuss the application, a tool you can use prior to the call to save time.

THE APPLICATION

Asking potential clients to complete an application prior to the phone call is part of my company's process. The application contains questions that enable us to get to know the client and his company or potential company. It enables us to determine if a potential client is interested in what we have to offer. After reviewing the application, we address any questions we might have before the phone call, as well as any concerns or objections the client might have.

By asking a potential client to set up a phone call and complete an application—and by us reviewing the application and addressing questions, concerns, or objections prior to the call—it ensures we're not talking to people on the phone who are going to waste our time, which ultimately increases closing percentages.

However, the application process is only part of the equation. If you want to make the sale, you must know how to structure the phone call and what to say to potential clients.

THE PRE-FRAME

The pre-frame is where the expectations for the phone call are set. The pre-frame is important because people get scared and freak out when they don't know what is going to happen. That's why people are scared to start a business—they don't know what will happen. That's why people are scared to invest—they don't know how the markets will respond and if they'll make or lose money. That's why people are scared of marriage—they don't know if they'll end up getting divorced.

The easiest way to understand a pre-frame is to look at a dating analogy. If I go on a date with a girl and our expectations are not lined up (she wants a relationship and I just want to hookup), the date won't go well. At some point, one of us will figure out we don't have the same expectations and the date will end. However, if we discuss our expectations prior to the date (pre-frame), both my date and I know what to expect if we proceed with the date.

By pre-framing a phone call with a potential client, you tell her exactly what's about to happen, because if she thinks something is going to happen and then it doesn't, you're not going to sell her. What happens on the call must align with what she's thinking.

Here's an example: I say, "Hey, Sally, so glad you're here. The goal of this call is to see how we can help you with your business, right? You're obviously on this call for a reason. You're not where you want to be. You're struggling, and our job is to see if we can help you figure out why that is and how to fix it. Okay? Now, by the end of the call, what we like to ask our potential clients to do is give us a yes or no decision. We don't say that to force you to do something you don't want to do, but we find that by the end of the call, if you're still not convinced we're a good fit, then you should just say no. If we can't convince you in an hour that we can help you grow your business, that means we didn't do a good job or we're not a good fit for you. So at the end of the call, after everything's been set on the table, I'll ask you if you feel confident and you can give me a yes or no decision."

Once we reach the end of the call, I bring back the pre-frame and say, "Do you remember at the beginning of the call, when you agreed to give me a yes or no? This is that time. So if you're not interested, you can tell me. If there's something concerning you, you can tell me that too. But at the end of the day, if you don't know what you should do right now, you probably should say no, because that means either we're not a fit or I haven't done a good job explaining, because most clients find that it's a no-brainer to work with me when they see my results."

If the answer is "yes," which it usually is, I'll say, "Great. Let's go ahead and dive in."

If the answer is "no," I'll say, "Let's reschedule when you're ready. In the meantime, I'll send you some homework videos to watch."

Pre-framing a call removes excuses from the equation. Each person knows what to expect going into the call.

Therefore, potential clients don't waste an hour of your time by hanging up on you at the end of the call instead of buying your services or product, or saying they'll get back to you when you know they won't. The pre-frame prevents you from wasting an hour with someone who is not prepared to make a decision. The pre-frame also gives potential clients "permission" to tell me after the call that they are not interested in purchasing what I'm selling (because I tell them this is an option during the pre-frame, and that makes potential clients think I have their best interests at heart, which I do). A salesman wants to make the sale at all costs. But you can't do it at the detriment of the potential client. If a client genuinely feels that we're not a good fit, he should also feel it's okay to tell me so. I think that's very important.

THE DISCOVERY QUESTIONS

It's a lot easier to convince someone to buy on the phone versus convincing them to buy via an online link from someone he doesn't know or trust. Phone sales allow you to address the 800 million excuses the client might have for not buying, figure out his objection (most people won't tell you their true objection), and then push the client into a corner and get him to make a decision.

Here's an example where I address a potential client's flawed logic.

The client says he can't afford it my coaching services.

I say in a nice way, "How much do you make in a month, if you don't mind me asking?"

He says, "I make $3,000."

"Okay, cool. So your plan is that you're going to save up money, right?"

He says, "Oh yeah, for sure, man. Like, as soon as I save money up, I'm going to buy from you."

I know this is total BS, that he's just lying to himself that his situation will change by continuing to do the same things that got him into the situation in the first place. But I don't tell him that outright. Instead, I say, "Okay, cool. Let's look at the math. How much is your rent?"

"About $1,500 per month."

"Okay, let's say between rent, groceries, and your other bills, you save about $400 a month. So six months from now, you've saved $2,500. The problem is that your car just broke down, so now you have to spend that money on your car. Six months later, your wife or girlfriend gets pregnant. Now you've got a kid to support. Look, I don't care what you do. But the reality is that the only way for you to get out of your current situation is to hire someone who knows more than you. And that's going to take an investment. So if you take one step back by spending this money with me, I'll help you take eight steps forward. You'll never have to worry about money again once I show you how to make it. But if you never jump on board and hire me, the job you're currently doing won't help you save the money you need. It's not about saving more. It's about making more. You're not going to get rich saving your money. You have to learn how to make more money. And then it becomes easy because you're making so dang much."

Discovery questions are designed to determine a potential client's goal and why he is on the phone call with you. For example, our prospective clients usually want to make more money, or in fewer cases, they have confidence issues when it comes to business dealings. Your prospective clients may have different goals depending on your specific online business.

It's important to understand not only the client's issue but also where it stems from. You need to break down the information so you understand the struggle. For example, is the client insecure because his wife left him? That's important to know. You don't want to use the information to manipulate him; you want to use it to guide him toward buying what you're selling. For example, I am where I am today because I didn't want to be a loser. At a finite level, that's reality. I wanted to become someone "important." That was my goal. That was why I hired my coaches.

Discovery questions for online business clients include:[5]

1. Why do you want to make a lot of money?
2. How much money do you want to make?
3. Why that amount?
4. Why does it matter?
5. Why are you struggling?
6. What's the problem?
7. What have you tried before?
8. Do you have any sales, marketing, or business experience?

Often people respond that they don't know the answers; they just know they want things to change. That's a BS reason. You need to dig further until you discover the real reason—it's the only way your call will be successful. Often, it's an insecurity issue, something they want to achieve in life but haven't been able to do for some reason, or something bad that happened in their life that is driving them to do better. Knowing this type of information is powerful and enables you to address it during the call. When you push on their pain, the chance that you close the sale is much higher.

---

5   These questions will be the same for most online business clients but can vary depending on the niche.

Here's an example: "Hey man, so your wife divorced you because you went into bankruptcy, and now that you have a new wife, you're about to go into bankruptcy again. What are the chances your new wife will divorce you too?"

I'm not trying to scare the prospective client. I'm pushing his buttons, so when he gets to the end of the call, he wants to purchase my services. It's important to note that if you don't talk about topics your potential client is interested in, he won't buy from you. It's like when you keep talking about Ferraris to someone and they don't care about fancy sports cars. They just want a reliable car.

Another example is when a potential fitness client told me he wanted to lose weight. I asked why.

He said, "Because I have low self-esteem."

Again, I asked, "Why?"[6]

He said, "Because my wife doesn't want to make love with me anymore because she thinks I look disgusting."

I know that hurt him, but it also motivated him to call me. He loved his wife and didn't want to lose her. Ultimately, he purchased my services so he could lose weight, get in shape, and keep his wife.

---

6   Usually you have to ask "Why?" a few times to dig deeper and discover someone's true issue.

If a dad wants to make money, I ask him why. He states he has seven kids. At the end of our phone call, if he gives me grief about purchasing my services, I'm going to throw the information back at him.

I'll say something like this: "I don't have kids like you. I'm not trying to say this is the correct stance, but what are your kids going to think if you decide not to do this and that's why you're not successful? Or are your kids just going to look you in the eye and say, 'Hey, you know what, Dad, it's okay that you didn't go through Tanner's program because we didn't really need the money that bad.' Is that okay with you? What if you can't afford your children's college or medical expenses? Is that okay with you, knowing you could have paid for it if you worked my program?"

Saying that to someone is powerful because it's reality. Many people may think it's harsh, but it's true. My calling is to help people, so I'll risk coming off as rude if it pushes that person to do something he may not have done otherwise. I needed that push as most of us do.

It's important to believe in what you're selling and bring that passion to the phone call. It's also important, as we discussed, to bring up a potential client's issues and what he cares about if you want to make closing the sale easier. At the end of the call, you'll have a loaded gun, which you previously filled with bullets (issues and concerns) that your potential client discussed during the call. Now, when a potential client complains about the cost of your services or goods, you have the ammunition you need to close the deal.

For example: "Remember when you said you were afraid your wife would divorce you if you declared bankruptcy again? If you don't purchase my program, how will you fix things?"

Discovery questions are powerful tools if you use them correctly. However, you must also understand the three pillars.

THE THREE PILLARS

The three pillars are three sales points you cover following the discovery questions that help convince someone why he should buy from you. The pillars can change depending on the offer. For each of my businesses, the three pillars stay the same, because I always sell the same thing. For our purposes, let's assume the phone call is with someone who is a more experienced online business owner:

1. For the first pillar, focus on what you can to do to help the client.

   I'll typically say, "We're going to craft and package together an offer that ensures you don't become a commodity. If you're selling soap or water or food at the end of the day, when it's all said and done, if you're selling the same thing as someone else, how does someone decide to buy?"

The client may say, "Whatever's cheaper."

"Right," I say. "So part of the reason you haven't been successful so far, Mike, is because every time you go to sell something, you're selling the same things as everyone else. That's why you think you can't charge more, because you're selling a commodity. But that's the problem. It's why Ferraris sell for approximately $250,000 and minivans sell for approximately $30,000. The minivan is a commodity and the Ferrari is not. There's more perceived value with the Ferrari. It's the same reason Nike can sell shoes for $160 and Payless sells them for $30. If your product or service is perceived as not being a commodity, it ensures respect in the marketplace and people will pay top dollar for it. There are a million people out there who will teach people how to build their business. I'm probably one of the most expensive, but people pay me all the time."

2. For the second pillar, focus on what you will provide to the client that will improve his circumstances.

I'll typically say, "We're going to create our unique mechanism for you called conversion conversations.

This is a unique method of follow-up texts, emails, voice messages, Facebook Messenger, etc. It's a system that I created that took my company from zero to eight figures in two years. Most coaches will tell you to run an ad to a webinar and that's all you have to do if you want to be rich. If that were true, why aren't more businesses successful in the online space? We need to create a system and a mechanism that will work no matter what, even if you have few marketing skills and you're new to this business, because at the end of the day, you're paying me to make you successful. And I have built a system that's easy to make work."

The key here is to build trust and tell them what you are going to do for them without giving the drilled-down specifics. You want to make the potential client hungry to purchase your product or services. Give them the "what," not the "how"—don't tell them how to do things; instead tell them what they need to do. Once they purchase your product or services, you show them the "how" and help them implement and execute it.

3. For the third pillar (my logical point), it's important to show the client the logic in paying for your product or service, and why your product or service is the way to go.

I'll typically say, "There are a million different business coaches out there that you can hire, but very few of them have built a seven-figure business-to-consumer business and a seven-figure business-to-business business. So isn't it more likely that I can help you if I've been successful in both markets, as opposed to some of those other coaches who coach without having built a business first?"

Once I've discussed the three pillars, I'll recap the information and also reiterate why I'm the best person to hire: I'm twenty-eight years old, I built a seven-figure business-to-consumer fitness company and a seven-figure business-to-business company in only twenty-two months, and I'm the only one to do that.

PROGRAM OVERVIEW

On this part of the sales call, review the program so the potential client knows the aspects it contains. Obviously, programs can vary, but I'll use mine as an example.

I'll typically say, "You have six group calls a week, and each call is led by a different expert in his field (copywriting, Facebook ads, sales, etc.). You also learn how to run ads, copywriting, sales, leadership, and messaging—basically all aspects of the business that you will need to know. Once the group calls are complete, you'll work with four full-time coaches on a one-to-one basis (we also have nine part-time coaches). You can message those coaches anytime you like on Facebook Messenger and also speak to them via Zoom as needed. The final part of the program is our portal, which contains step-by-step videos showing you everything you need to know to make your business a success. So to sum up, there are three elements: group coaching calls, unlimited one-to-one access to your coaches, and the portal."

It's important to keep the program overview section of the call brief. People don't buy because of benefits or features. They buy because they trust you and believe in your three pillars.

EXPECTATIONS

To avoid misunderstanding, it's important to set expectations. Setting expectations informs potential clients what they will receive if they purchase my services. It also focuses on explaining the difficulties in learning how to operate an online business.

When setting expectations, I'll typically say, "The first thing to understand is that this process is going to be really hard. Even though I've told you that you can make a lot of money, at the end of the day, if it were easy to become a millionaire, more people would be millionaires, right? You need to understand that we will show you the path, but it will be harder for you than someone who has been in business for two years or longer. If you come into my program and start comparing yourself to other people who've been in business longer, you'll feel frustrated and it won't be fun for you. Although you'll learn the necessary tools and I'll tell you exactly what to do, it will still be hard.[7]

"The second thing you need to understand is that your ability to succeed will be determined by how quickly you learn new skills and implement them. Does that make sense? Great.

"The third thing to understand is that this program will cost a lot of money. Now I know that's not fun to hear. I know you didn't get on this call expecting to think, 'Oh my gosh, I can't wait to give Tanner all my money.' But understand that I spent almost half a million dollars on coaching and millions of dollars on Facebook ads, and I struggled and struggled for years and years. You're coming into the program and learning everything I've learned for a fraction of the cost. Is the program expensive? Sure. But there are very few places where you can learn all of this for what I'm charging. If I provide everything I promise, it's expensive because otherwise I can't afford to offer you one-to-one support. I can't teach you everything I've promised and make it cheap."

---

7   If I don't tell them how difficult it will be, if I don't bring back some sense of reality, I will sound like some rich scheme guru and the potential client will think, "This is too good to be true."

PRICE DROP

In this portion of the sales call, explain the specifics of what you are selling (the length of a coaching program, for example) and the typical price. Then offer a price drop. Some sales trainers will disagree with a price drop, and I've even had some of my own sales reps stop using it, depending on the sophistication of the buyer.[8] Price drops are what I used to quickly build my business. They're effective and lead to sales.

Here's what I might say: "The program is four months for twelve grand. As long as you put down a minimum deposit today, that price will drop by two grand. The reason is twofold. The first reason is to incentivize you to sign up; I want you to make a decision. I found that by the end of a phone call, if someone still doesn't know what to do, he's probably never going to work with me. Of course, there are always exceptions. The second reason is because successful online businesses spend an exorbitant amount of money on marketing. I want to make sure I'm collecting money as fast as possible so that my business can continue to grow and be successful. I know you don't care about my business, but I want to be transparent and honest with you. So that's how much it costs and that's how it will work. Tell me your thoughts."

---

8 If a client is brand-new to purchasing services online, the price drop will typically work. For others, it may not.

There are a million ways to close, and it's up to you how you do it. But once you close, remain quiet and let the other person respond.

If the potential client states he has to think about whether he wants to buy, which is one of the biggest issues you will face, I'll respond with this: "I'm not trying to force you to do something you don't want to do, but the discount simply holds your spot. You can change your mind. But if you're not even willing to do that, that shows me you may not be as serious as you're saying."

HANDLING OBJECTIONS OR REBUTTALS

When you're on a sales call and the potential client objects to something, acknowledge it, no matter what he said. For example, if he states he doesn't want to sign up for your program or services because his kids need braces, tell him you understand. Then return to and address his pain.

I'll typically say something like this: "I totally hear what you're saying, but if you remember earlier in the call, you said X, Y, and Z, right?" (This is where you bring up everything he told you earlier in the call: scared to go bankrupt again, scared his wife will divorce him if his business fails, etc.).

When he acknowledges that he said those things, I say, "If

that's true, then the only thing left for you to do is to sign up for my coaching."

The following image represents this last aspect of the sales call. You keep working the preceding steps, circling through them on the clock, until you close the deal and make the sale. Many sales guys won't address new objections once they've cycled through the process once, and therefore they lose the sale. You must continue to address the objections until the prospective client no longer has a reason to say no.

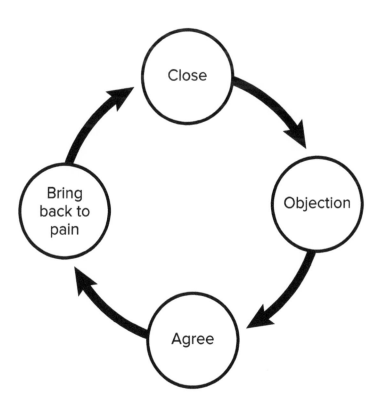

Phone sales are an important tool that can yield large sales in a short period of time. However, they must be done correctly if you want them to be successful.

You also need to understand how to use ads if you want to drive up sales.

CHAPTER 8

ADS

You can use phone calls without using ads. But when you use both tools, it's a powerful combination.

When two of my first clients hired me to coach them, their online fitness training business was making $3,000 a month. During our first days of working together, and without spending money on ads, they made $10,000. Once they began using ads, their income jumped substantially. They saw a six-times return on investment (ROI), meaning for every $5,000 they spent, they made $30,000.

Two fitness trainers I also coached, Morgan and Jessica,[9] went from making $10,000 without spending money on ads to making $25,000 for every $5,000 they spent on ads, giving them a five-times ROI. Once they realized the power

9   Jessica's name has been changed to protect her privacy.

of ads, they continued to use them, and their business grew and has grown consistently.

A third client, Josh, who ran an Amazon FBA[10] offer, was making between $15,000 and $30,000 a year and didn't know how to grow his business. Once he learned how to run ads and began using them, he started making over $100,000 a month within three months.

If you spend a dollar and make two or more back, that's a good deal. My business relies on ads; that's how I get people to know about our services. Think about why most businesses fail. Nobody knows they exist, and therefore they can't get the customers they need. Ads introduce new customers—who will then go through my sales process and purchase my services—to my company. Because my advertising ROI is high, I make a lot of money, which enables me to expand my business, build a bigger team, and work with additional clients. As long as I continue to run ads and receive a good ROI, I can grow my company as large as I want.

Often, people think they will become rich simply by running ads, but it's important to remember that ads are only part of the process. What happens after the ad (the phone call described in the previous chapter) is the magic; that's where the money is made. Ads are the gasoline you add to

---

10 FBA is fulfillment by Amazon—where you sell products on Amazon to make money.

the fire that makes your business grow. Without ads, the fire will die because you won't raise awareness regarding your business and therefore won't have an opportunity to make sales.

But you must know how to run ads properly to achieve good results—and without spending a lot of money. Otherwise, you're just wasting time and money.

Some will argue that organic growth is best because you aren't spending money to reach people. However, organic growth will always limit the size of your business. New people won't be able to find out about your company fast enough for it to grow extremely large—unless you use paid methods.

CAMPAIGN

A campaign is the way you use advertising to reach your target audience. And each type of ad campaign has its own objectives, which are actions you want your ad to entice potential clients to take. For example, video or engagement ads simply require the potential client to click to see a video or go to a landing page. Conversion ads[11] offer a bigger commitment from the potential client. When they

---

11   When someone buys something or becomes a lead, meaning they gave you their email as a result of the ad.

see your conversion ad, potential clients may be enticed to
do one of the following:

- Book a sales phone call.
- Register for a webinar.
- Opt in to an email list.
- Buy a low-ticket (lower-priced) item.

It's important to determine your objective before running
an ad because Facebook, which is the easiest and best platform to use for beginners, optimizes ad reach based on the
type of ad used. If the campaign level is video ads, Facebook
will show the ad to people who view a lot of videos. If the
campaign level is conversion ads, Facebook will show the
ad to people who buy things.

In looking at ad pricing, you may think it's best to use
video view ads because they're cheaper than conversion
ads. Because conversion ads are designed to get people to
purchase items or services, they're the most highly used
and the costliest. Using video view ads instead of conversion ads is a huge mistake. You're wasting money instead
of saving it, because Facebook will only show video view
ads to people who watch videos, and not to people who
purchase things. Your ad won't be seen by the right people:
those who buy from ads.

Conversion ads are, however, the proper campaign level

for Facebook if your objective is to make a sale. To learn more about using conversion ads on other social media platforms such as Instagram or LinkedIn and even ones you haven't heard of, contact me and my team at https://www.infiniteincomebook.com/info.

AD SET

Ad set is who you're going to show an ad to and how much you're going to spend on the ad. The first aspect is telling Facebook (or other ad platforms) who might be interested in what you're selling, so that Facebook knows the target of your ad.

It's simple to determine who should see your ad. Ask yourself:

1. Who are your potential clients?[12]
2. What are your potential clients interested in?
3. What types of jobs do your potential clients have?

For example, I have a client who teaches people how to build Amazon e-commerce businesses. He might tell Facebook that he wants his ad to be seen by people who have an interest in Amazon, Jeff Bezos (because he owns Amazon), entrepreneurship (because that's an entre-

---

12   If you want to offer a localized service, you can choose from the ad set options to limit your ads to be seen by those who live in a five-mile radius, for example, versus nationwide.

preneurship type of business), drop shipping (because Amazon does a lot of drop shipping), and e-commerce (because Amazon is an e-commerce business).

The second aspect in determining ad set is deciding how much you are willing to spend. I would suggest beginners spend the maximum amount they are willing to pay for a lead. A lead for our purposes is when someone provides his email. So if I'm offering fitness services with my ad, the most I'm going to spend per lead is $10.

For a business-to-consumer ad, aim for a 2 percent–plus click-through rate. Click-through rate is how many people out of 100 click your ad and go to the next page. So, for every 100 impressions (people who view your ad), you want two or more people clicking on that ad,[13] which you hope will turn into leads. For a business-to-business ad, aim for a 1 percent or higher click-through rate. Keep in mind that these click-through rates are guidelines for beginners, not rules. I couldn't give you hard numbers unless I was getting down and dirty with you in a one-to-one coaching setting; the best I can do here is to give guidelines.

If I don't get a lead for a consumer-to-consumer offer for $10 (maximum $15), I'll turn off the ad. I'm either targeting the wrong audience, targeting the wrong interests, running an ineffective ad, etc. If I'm in a business-to-business offer,

---

13   Two percent is about normal.

I might spend $20. (If you're using ManyChat, double the cost;[14] if ManyChat is unfamiliar to you because you're a beginner running an online business, don't worry about it for now).

Keep in mind that if you run twenty ad sets, not every ad will work, no matter how targeted it is. Running ads is like going to the casino. Are you going to win every hand? No, of course not. Ads are calculated gambling. You are determining that if you spend a certain amount of money and target your ad to a specific audience, you will probably get a lead.

Once you run an ad, see what works and what doesn't. If an ad works, double down on it by continuing to run it and investing more money while trying to find additional interests that would entice like-minded people to buy your product or service.

You might be thinking you don't have a lot of money to spend on ads because you're not making a lot of money. If you had $1 million in the bank or unlimited income, it wouldn't matter how much you spent on ads. You could

---

14 When people click the ad, ManyChat activates Facebook Messenger. However, only some people will go to your landing page because you can't send them there automatically from Messenger; they have to deliberately click another link to do it. Because there is an additional step involved (clicking through to the landing page from Messenger) when using ManyChat, you lose potential clients in the process, so it doubles your lead cost. However, if you use my ultra-effective method of conversion conversations, you will make more sales when using ManyChat, because you will be able to follow up *every single lead* and not just those who click through to your landing page (approximately 50 percent of those who click the ad).

spend and spend, however much it cost you to get a lead. But when you're starting an online business, if you pay too much to get a lead, you won't make more money than you spend. You must set thresholds and limits regarding how much you are willing to spend on ads so that you make money instead of losing it.

The rule of thumb for ad spending is to spend only as much money as you are willing to lose. For a beginner, if you can't spend at least $3,000 a month or $100 per day, you're not ready to run ads (in my opinion). Ten dollars is the average cost for a lead. If you spend $100 per day, that provides only ten leads per day. If you get only ten leads per day, you get only three hundred leads per month. Of those, probably only fifteen will lead to phone calls, where you then have the opportunity to sell to your customer. If you spend only $2 a day, it's not enough to generate the leads you need, and it's a waste of time and money. If that's all you can afford, focus on organic (free) efforts instead of running ads, such as messaging people on Facebook and Instagram, connecting to those on your email list, and using referrals to obtain contacts.

Keep in mind that not every lead turns into a call, and not every call turns into a sale. As you grow your business, know the average numbers you're looking for (average lead cost, average application cost, and average client acquisition cost) so your growth is predictable.

Tips for running ads:

1. If your ad isn't working, don't freak out. Change who you are targeting and/or their interests.
2. Remember that ad success is based on who sees your ad (i.e., the right people), what time of day they see it, and if those viewing your ad click on the ad.
3. Ads won't work forever. I employ a full-time ad manager who changes my ad sets in some way every day. Typically, ad sets will have a shelf life of twenty-four to seventy-two hours or less (sometimes longer, but I'm giving you a general rule). After that, the ad needs to be changed.

VIDEO VS. IMAGES

Both video and images work well as advertising tools; however, video ads are more entertaining. For beginning advertisers, it's best to use images because it's easier and faster to create an image than to shoot, edit, and post a video. In addition, if a social media platform like Facebook doesn't like the video, the platform will take it down. If that happens, you've spent all that time and done all that work for nothing. Stick with using images in your ads and move into using videos once your business has grown (and you have a team to help you create them). This will free up your time to focus on other aspects of the business while still enabling you to achieve success through advertising.

THE WHOA FACTOR

A good ad, whether it is a video or an image, must have a whoa factor. It's the difference between seeing a cat walking down the street and a cat jumping on a trampoline and doing flips. Seeing a cat walking down the street is not very interesting, but seeing a cat doing flips on a trampoline catches your attention. When I started my fitness business, I crushed it because my ad featured an image of me shirtless, and I was in really good shape. It made people stop and take a look.

The written information in your image or video ad contains five parts that lead up to the call to action—or what you want the potential client to do when they see your ad:

1. The first part should address the target audience. For example, if the ad is targeting dancers, the first sentence would say something like "Attention Dancers."
2. The second part should address a pain point. For example: "Have you ever struggled to dance again after injury?"
3. The third part should cover your story and how you relate. For example: "I can totally relate because when I was twelve, I broke my leg and couldn't dance for a long time. When it was time to dance again, I struggled because my body no longer moved the way it had previously."
4. The fourth part should cover your epiphany—how you

resolved the problem and became successful. This is where you give them the "secret sauce" or epiphany you had: Why buy your stuff over anyone else's? What sets you apart? How you describe it is super important. If the potential client thinks he knows what you are selling or can easily obtain it, he isn't going to buy it. Here's a good example of what to say: "I realized with the help of my trainer that my muscles were tight because they hadn't moved for so long and that my body was still compensating for the injury despite its having healed. After learning a series of stretches and exercises that are widely unknown and implementing them, I became a prima ballerina for a prestigious dance company and traveled the world for years. Now I've settled down and I'm living my dream making money while helping others return to dance after injury."

5. The fifth part should be the call to action. For example: "If you're tired of not doing what you love, of not being able to dance, and you want to learn how to teach your body how to move properly and ultimately dance without risking reinjury using these special techniques, click on the link below."

Video ads should be short. When creating a video ad, it's best to keep it under sixty seconds. People have short attention spans, and you don't want them to click away from your ad before it reaches the call to action.

I run a lot of ads and the format always remains the same. However, the content changes: the setting, what I'm saying, and the story.

In a video ad for fitness coaching, I might say, "Are you someone who looks terrible and has no confidence? If so, I know how you feel. When I was a little kid, I was bullied and others made fun of me a lot. Because of that, I really wanted to learn how to get in shape so I could make them stop. I tried a bunch of different diets and workout programs, but they never worked until I finally figured out the special 'X' diet and program. Ever since, I've been in great shape. I tried many different diets and programs before I found success, but once I figured out what actually worked—the 'X' diet and program—it changed my life. Now I show people how to do it. So if you want to look good, stop being insecure, and learn how I got in shape, click the link below."

In an ad geared toward business owners, I might say, "Hey, are you a business owner? Are you a person who wants to build an online business, but you don't know how? I totally understand the frustration, because back in the day I paid five coaches thousands of dollars and I got nothing to show for it until I figured out a secret mechanism called conversion conversations. That helped take my company from zero to eight figures in just two years. If you want to learn how to use conversion conversations and make a lot of money, click on the link below."

Nike is a company that uses few words to convey a strong message in its sneaker ads, and it does it right. In each ad, the company focuses on athletes and their problems, such as perseverance or adversity. Then the ads present a call to action—Just Do It! Once the athletes heed the call to action, they succeed. Whenever I see a Nike ad and hear that call to action, I get chills and go buy their sneakers, because I can relate to the struggling athletes in the ad and their ultimate success.

Now that you know what makes a good ad, you also need to understand retargeting.

RETARGETING

Retargeting is reshowing an ad to someone (who has landed on a specific page after clicking on the ad) in an attempt to convince him to buy. Most people don't buy after seeing only one ad. It can take seven ads, or five ads and three emails, for example, for that person to purchase your product or services. If you saw my ad and never saw anything from me again, you probably wouldn't buy from me. But if over the next seven days, you saw an ad every single day, you'd start to ask yourself questions—"What is this about? Who is this guy? What does he do?"—and you're more likely to buy. That's the power of retargeting ads.

Retargeting ads can be set up to target potential clients or buyers automatically. On Facebook, for example, I instruct Facebook to send a specific retargeting ad to anyone who lands on page "A" but doesn't land on page "B," meaning they left the page and didn't click through any further. I also tell Facebook to send a specific retargeting ad to anyone who lands on the first two pages but doesn't land on the third page. Lastly, I tell Facebook to send a specific retargeting ad to anyone who lands on all three pages but who doesn't buy. Each ad is specific to the action taken (landing on one, two, or three pages). This is just a general example. You can retarget page engagers, likers, email lists, purchasers, etc.—the options are unlimited.

I generally recommend retargeting the most in the seven days after a potential client lands on one of your pages—that ensures the potential client has seen it. It's also typically when you see the most results. You can use each retargeting ad for as long as you want, but the further out you target, the less effective it becomes. If he hasn't taken action within a month, he probably won't.

Retargeting ads maximize your ad spend. It's a lot cheaper to retarget than to run ads to cold traffic, because the retargeting audience is smaller than the general audience. For example, if your initial ad is seen by 10 million people, you may need to retarget only 10,000, so the cost is not as great.

Here are some sample retargeting ads:

- "Hey [insert person's name here], I saw you clicked on my ad. Thanks so much, but because you didn't purchase my book, I'm giving you another opportunity to buy it."
- "Hey [insert person's name here], I saw that you went to my page earlier and thought about booking a call but didn't. There are usually three reasons why someone doesn't do that [and then I go through those three reasons]. Don't worry, I'll take good care of it. Go ahead and click the link, and I'll see you on the other side." (This type of ad is used when you get a lead but the person doesn't book a phone call).

Ads are the key to success online. If you can learn to run a successful ad, you can make a lot of money.

As you can see, if you use ads successfully, you will obtain quick results and have the potential to become infinitely wealthy.

But there's also another important tool in your toolbox that you need to know how to use.

CHAPTER 9

FUNNELS

When I started my business, I thought I needed a fancy and expensive website. My mentor spent time teaching me how to build it—the tech, the software, the automations—and how to create an email list, but it didn't help me generate sales. After two years learning those skills (with his help and on my own), I had no money to show for my efforts. It was insane.

I created four website pages (a sales page, an upsell[15] page, another upsell page, and a downsell[16] page). Creating sales

---

15 Convincing someone to purchase additional products or services for an added cost. For example: "You can get my book; it's free plus shipping. You can also get the audio book for an additional twenty dollars. And if you want the coffee mug that goes with it, that's an extra twenty-five dollars."

16 Offering an alternate product or service at a lower price to someone who doesn't purchase your high-end product or service. For example: On my website, if I'm trying to sell you my audiobook for twenty dollars but you don't buy, I'll immediately try to sell you something that's cheaper, such as a sticker for ten dollars or a bookmark for three dollars.

pages takes a long time and they're lengthy. My sales page contained as much information as a ten-page book. It's a lot of work. And it was overkill. It wasn't the right place for me to start. If you want to become a writer, you don't start off writing a three-hundred-page book. You start off writing a short story or an essay. The same thing applies to an online business.

As a beginner in the online business space and in running a business in general, my mentor advised me to work on the hardest thing possible instead of working on what would make me money. Learning how to design a website and create a mailing list were not the skills I needed to know when starting my online business. The process, however, became beneficial down the road, once I learned how to run ads and make sales.

I'd trusted that my mentor had my best interests at heart, and he did. Because he is very experienced and had run a business for more than twenty years, he'd had success doing what he showed me—building a website and using it to make sales. However, he'd never sold high-ticket items, and I was inexperienced and not in a position financially or market-skills-wise to make it work.

You might think that people typically look for a website to legitimize a business. That may be correct, but what they really want to know is if they can get results. For example, if you're selling a fitness product, a potential client could look at a picture of you on social media or on a website landing page and, because you are fit, know that you understand how to get in shape. That will lead to a sale.

When most people think of websites, they imagine menu tabs. For example, Amazon's menu tabs include Whole Foods, Today's Deals, Best Sellers, etc. Most online businesses that are selling services, especially those starting out, don't need a fancy website. They need only a single landing page that tells the viewer information about the business and contains client testimonials and a call to action (sign up for a free phone call, for example).

Today, my businesses have websites, but I don't send people to them in an effort to make sales. I send people to the websites to read my life story or to view client testimonials.

Funnels, which are used to increase sales, are more important than fancy and expensive websites.

WHAT IS A FUNNEL?

A funnel is a predictable customer journey, usually occurring as the result of viewing an ad. The funnel takes a potential client through a process rather than enabling him to randomly click around a website and hopefully buy. Funnels are created with the intent of getting someone to take a specific action, as opposed to browsing.

In a funnel, the client lands on page one (the landing page), which sends him to page two and then page three, etc. It's a specific journey, and every client who views your funnel takes it. One hundred people may view the first page, but of those, only a certain number will click through to the second page, the third, etc. Regardless of how far through each person clicks, a funnel controls the process from beginning to end.

Funnels are more effective than websites in general because funnels present several limited options versus many. It's like going to a restaurant and being forced to choose between one menu item or leaving the restaurant (a funnel) versus choosing from three hundred menu items (a general website). Statistically, when someone is presented with limited choices, he is more likely to buy because he won't be overwhelmed by the decision-making process.

Using funnels creates predictable income by employing a process that often converts to a sale. Even if a potential client fails to complete the funnel and clicks away from it after providing an email, there is an opportunity to retarget the client with a new ad. In comparison, a website does not provide the same opportunity, so the potential sale is lost.

PAGES OF A FUNNEL

The content on each page of a funnel is dependent on the funnel and what you want to accomplish. Here's an example:

- First Page: This page is the landing page. It should be simple and contain one objective and a call to action. Everything on the page should push the viewer to make a choice and to take action. For example: "Hey, click below to get my secrets to book writing. Provide your email and I'll send you a PDF." The elements of a first page/landing page are the headline, the sub headline, a video or text, and a place to insert an email address or book a phone call.
- Second Page: This page appears as soon as someone provides his email. It might either be an offer to purchase services or to book a phone call, depending on what you are selling.
- Third Page: This page often contains an upsell (and is followed by one or two additional upsell pages), if the product you are selling is inexpensive. Or the page can contain a "thank you" to prep a potential client for a phone call.

A thank you page might say, "Cool. You're booked for the call. Be sure to watch these videos first. Also, here are some frequently asked questions."

By providing potential clients with videos to watch prior to a phone call, it leads them to think the way you want—about buying—and you're not wasting time on the phone call discussing material you provide in the videos. If I'm selling my coaching services, for example, I'll provide potential clients with videos that relate to their current situation, such as these: Have You Worked with Anyone Like Me Before?; Have You Already Spent Money on a Coach or a Course?; Are You Willing to Invest?; Stop Paying for the Wrong Coaches—How to Choose the Right Coach; Why I Always Have Debt; Do You Value Time or Money More?; Are You a Business Hypocrite?; Do You Have a Faucet System? (a system to bring you leads on demand); You Don't Need a Big Following to Make Money; If You Don't Have One-on-One Coaching, They Don't Care About You, etc. Each video is short—three to six minutes in length.

You may be wondering how the technology behind funnels work. There are two ways:

1. ClickFunnels (the software company I use) tracks page views and stats for you so you don't have to.
2. Using a Facebook pixel when running Facebook ads. Each page of the funnel contains a Facebook pixel (that you have to insert manually) that lets Facebook know that the person took a specific action, which is super important when reading data on your Facebook

ads. So if someone clicks on the first page and enters his email, the pixel lets Facebook know that someone was on that page and then went to the second page. If someone books a call, the pixel on that page lets Facebook know that he was there as well. A Facebook pixel is simply a piece of code you place on a website. Think of it like a stamp or sticker you place on every car you see as you walk down the street. If everyone knows you place blue stickers on every car you see, then when they see the stickers, they'll know you had been there. Pixels are the same; they leave a digital footprint every time someone takes a specific action, which enables you to know if your marketing is working. Imagine running ads without receiving any resulting data; it would be like throwing money off the balcony and praying more would just come to you. Nothing is in your control.

LOW-TICKET VS. HIGH-TICKET FUNNELS

A low-ticket funnel is used to sell something that is cheap. In comparison, a high-ticket funnel is used to sell something that is expensive.

If you're reading this book, you're probably new to the online space and not running a seven-figure business. Therefore, it's best if you use high-ticket funnels, because you don't have the profit margin to sell low-ticket offers.

If you sell a low-ticket offer such as a $20 book, it may cost you $50 in ads to do so. That means you lose $30 for every book sold. In addition, if you have only $5,000 to spend on advertising, you can't afford to lose money. That's a model for expert marketers and not for beginners. You won't make any money and you'll go broke. Even if you offer a low-ticket funnel without running ads and you're selling your book for $20, you need to sell thousands of books to make a lot of money.

If, on the other hand, you sell a high-ticket offer[17] such as a $6,000 program, and the advertising costs you your entire ad budget of $5,000, you will still make a profit of $1,000 if you sell only one program. And that's the worst-case scenario—that should never happen. Realistically, after spending $5,000 on advertising, you should sell two to three programs, making a lot of profit that you can start utilizing. You're giving yourself a chance to succeed, and you make money faster.

Marketing is why people invest in high-ticket products. It convinces them you are better than everyone else. If you can convince someone that what you have to teach is unavailable anywhere else or that you are superior to other

---

17 You should always sell something you are good at or pay a coach to help you figure out what that is if you don't already know. Being considered an expert in your field enables you to command a high price.

coaches, they will pay for your services. It's all about perceived value.

There are very few people who sell straight low-ticket sales and do so successfully, unless they have a lot of clout like Russell Brunson. If, as a new business owner, I spend $100,000 on advertising high-ticket sales and make $400,000, that's a four-times ROI. If I spend the same $100,000 on advertising low-ticket sales and make $50,000, I've lost money. The point of spending $100,000 and losing $5,000 is to obtain qualified buyers who are more likely to purchase your high-ticket program. For example, if out of those who purchased $50,000 of your services, you have twenty who also purchase a $10,000 course, then you actually make money (20 buyers × $10,000 = $200,000). Use low-ticket funnels to generate low-ticket sales when you can temporarily afford to lose money, knowing that ninety days down the road, you will be able to leverage those sales into high-ticket sales.

Here's an example of how I use a low-ticket funnel to sell programs that teach clients how to operate an online business: If I sell a $97 program and the client buys that program, I will attempt to upsell a $197 program. Each program gives the client an additional piece he needs to build an online business. If the client buys the $197 program, I'll attempt to upsell a $997 program. My goal is to nurture him and get him to buy my high-ticket program, which can range from $3,000 to $20,000. The $197 and $997 programs are one-time upsells. If he doesn't buy right then, the offer is no longer available. If the client doesn't buy any of the programs, I'll attempt to downsell him something. If he doesn't buy that either, I'll use retargeting ads. The purpose of the funnel is to get him to buy something, and if he has a good experience, hopefully he'll buy something more expensive down the line.

Once you become experienced with funnels and advertising, and you are making a substantial amount of money, you can use low-ticket funnels to sell a lower-priced product and later leverage that into high-ticket sales. For example, if I sell $50,000 in low-ticket offers and later upsell the same number of people to make an additional $400,000, I've made $450,000 for $100,000 I've spent on ads. That grows the business substantially.

As your business grows, so does the cost of doing business. As a result, you must sell high-ticket items in order to remain profitable. In addition, the cost of high-ticket advertising is greater than the cost of low-ticket advertising, so you will have to make up that cost in sales.

WHEN FUNNELS DON'T WORK

What happens when someone clicks away from your landing page and doesn't give you his email address? Or he doesn't book a phone call? You need to figure out what's not working by looking at the stats; it's all in the numbers. Ideally you want a 3 percent conversion rate. If you're only getting a 0.3 percent conversion rate, that sucks. Either the wording or the video is not working. You must change one element or the other and try again. If it's still not working, you must systematically make changes until you succeed.[18] That's why funnels are so difficult—you're guessing at the problem, and each time you fix something and try again, it's time-consuming and expensive. My process of conversion conversations removes the pressure to make funnels work. If someone signs up for my services through a funnel, great. If he doesn't, I'll message him and get him to sign up that way.

EMAIL STRATEGY WITHIN YOUR FUNNEL

Once a potential client provides an email, it's important to follow up with a seven-to-ten-day email sequence that pushes him to take action. If, for example, you want him to buy something, write emails that get him to buy that item. The emails should talk directly to him and tell him what you want him to do. You might even address potential objections he may have, concerns, or a similar client. For example, if a client says he's scared of investing $10,000, I'll say, "Janice was the same way, and now she's making

---

18   The issue could also be something as simple as a button color; statistics show that an orange button color works better than any other color.

a shitload of money." The point is to get him to take the action you want him to take. The longer someone doesn't take action, the less likely he is to do so. It's like seeing a beautiful girl and not asking her out right away. If you don't ask her out, you're not going to ask her out three weeks later. You might think about it for a few days and then move on to something else. In addition, the longer someone goes without taking action, the more likely he is to forget about you and your offer. People have short attention spans. They have busy lives. They don't necessarily care about what you're selling, and they'll forget about your offer. You must hit them fast if you want them to buy.

It typically takes seven to nine impressions for someone to buy something. That means you need to see my offer seven to nine times before you will buy. If someone provides his email and I email him in that initial seven-to-ten-day window, I'm making another impression. If I wait until two months have passed, it's not that they won't buy, but it becomes less likely.

As you can see, you don't need a fancy website for your online business, especially when you're just starting out. What's important for success are the funnels you create and how you use them.

CONCLUSION

The internet is here to stay, and everything is moving online. Amazon is one of the biggest companies in the world. Airbnb is 100 percent online. Uber and Uber Eats aren't going anywhere. Some of the biggest companies are online.

Now is the perfect time to start your online business. Having an online business gives you the potential to earn a six-figure-plus income and the freedom and time to do the things you love outside of work.

Anyone can start an online business once you know how. But if you want to achieve success, you must have personal skills, such as determination and perseverance, and an understanding of and willingness to implement the practical tools for building an online business.

Now that I've shown you the basics to build your online business and you have a blueprint of what to follow and what to look for, you don't have to make the same mistakes I made.

What are you waiting for?

Do you want to be poor for another week?

Or do you want to run an online business that gives you the potential for a six-figure income and also gives you the money and the freedom to live the life of your dreams?

I live the life of my dreams. I travel a lot while still making $1 million-plus per month, live in a 5,000-square-foot penthouse, own two expensive cars that I paid for in full, spent time in Africa building a school for kids, paid off my parents' mortgage, and helped pay for my aunt's medical bills.

I'm no longer working crazy hours, six days a week, selling door-to-door, busting my butt, and not having anything to show for it. Now I work a few hours a day and have fun in my life. I can buy things, travel, give the money to charity—do what I want to do when I want—while not having to worry if I can pay the bills. Instead of feeling depressed, discouraged, upset, angry, and hopeless, like I used to, I now feel relieved, happy, ecstatic, proud, courageous, and stress-free. I'm excited about what life has to offer, and I enjoy each day. I went from being bullied and having no options to being able to do whatever I want with whoever I want, whenever I feel like it. That's pretty cool.

And it's all because I started an online business.

You can do it too!

If you need additional help in starting your online business or improving sales for your current online business, get in touch with me and my team at https://www.infiniteincome book.com/info.

If you want to use the systems and resources I use, go to https://www.infiniteincomebook.com/resources for more information.

SCAN ME

ACKNOWLEDGMENTS

Mom, thank you for being good to me even when I didn't deserve it. Thank you for driving me around, making 300 homemade meals a day so I could gain weight for sports, and encouraging me as a young man.

I know I wasn't the easiest child to deal with, and as I've grown older, I am in awe at how many things you did for me that most parents don't do.

No matter what obstacles I have overcome, they would have been infinitely harder without your love and care. Thank you for always loving me unconditionally and for having more patience than any other person I've ever met. God knows you needed it to deal with my teenager attitude growing up.

I love you.

Dad, thank you for teaching me how to be a man and how to work hard. As I've gotten older, I've realized how few people even know what hard work looks like. Seeing you take care of our family with seven kids on a teacher's salary was nothing short of inspiring.

I remember you'd cut grass, power-wash neighbors' driveways, and do anything extra you had to do to make sure we always had enough money and didn't go without.

As a kid, it was hard to appreciate it, but now, as a man, I realize how lucky I was. In today's societies, families are missing responsible men who will stick it out and provide for their wife and kids no matter what. Thank you for always treating my mother with respect and for always doing your best. Even when I disagreed with you, I knew deep down you were doing what you thought was best for our family.

Most families are broken, and more kids than ever before are growing up without a caring father to show them how to work hard and treat others with respect. Thank you for teaching me those things.

Thank you for being hard on me. Thank you for holding me to a high standard of excellence and for not just giving me anything I asked for while growing up.

If you had, I would not possess the drive I have today. Instead, I would have settled for mediocrity, always knowing that my dad would come to the rescue. I'm so glad you taught me tough life lessons early on so I wouldn't have to learn them later in life.

Thank you for teaching me that you can have anything in life you want if you're willing to work for it. That nobody owes you anything, but that anything is possible.

Without these lessons, I never would have had the determination to defy all odds and create a life that most told me was just a pipe dream.

I'll be forever grateful to you for the lessons you taught me that have made me financially successful beyond my wildest dreams.

It makes me happy to know I can take care of you and Mom in your old age like you took care of me as a kid.

I love you.

To David Frey, I wouldn't be writing this book today without you. You took me in and mentored me with no benefit to yourself. You taught me everything you knew about online marketing to give me the starting help I needed.

If it wasn't for you, I'd be working some nine-to-five job, hoping that life would get better someday.

I am so blessed to have met you, to have been taught by you, and to have grown a friendship with you. You're the closest thing to a second father figure that I have. You've always looked out for me, and you've always given me advice with my best interests in mind.

Thank you for giving me a chance to become someone and for being the only person who believed in me when I started this thing. Neither my parents nor siblings initially did that, but you did. You saw something in me that I couldn't see yet.

You talked me out of quitting more than five times in a three-year period while I was struggling to get things off the ground. Without you, I probably would have quit, because at times things felt unbearable.

I respect who you are as a person and for what you believe in. I know when you originally said you would mentor me, it was with the hope that I'd become more spiritual. I know that you place God and family above all else, including money. I respect you for that. I know I may not be in the place spiritually that you had hoped for me, but I promise I will always try to be the best man I can be.

Money has allowed me to do things and help others in ways

I had never thought possible. Thank you for helping me acquire the skills I needed to make this dream a reality.

I truly will be sad when you are no longer on this earth, and I hope that we can continue to make memorable moments together over the coming years.

I love you.

Benson and Gentry, thank you both for becoming my first workers with not much more than a promise that I would make sure your bills were paid.

I know when we started this thing that it was probably scary for you to leave school and go all in on this with me, not knowing what the future would hold.

I'm so happy I had and have you guys. You're both hard workers, and I know I can always trust you.

This journey has been so much more fun with you by my side. I hope you guys know I love you and I will always have your backs.

I can't wait to see what the future holds for us.

Love you both.

ABOUT THE AUTHOR

TANNER CHIDESTER, the CEO and founder of EliteCEOs.com, built his multimillion-dollar online company from scratch in under three years with no budget, marketing plan, or business experience. With few resources of his own and after working with multiple business coaches whose advice didn't lead him to financial success, he discovered the element every online business needs to succeed—conversion conversations. Now he empowers all types of entrepreneurs, from realtors and writers to personal trainers and consultants, to take control of their lives and gain financial independence, flexibility, and personal freedom. In his customizable approach, Tanner teaches entrepreneurs how to build their own online empires using the same strategies he employed, such as establishing sales funnels, creating and leveraging social media ads, and using conversion conversations. Tanner has received four

Two Comma Club Awards (after making $1,000,000 in revenue in his first twelve months in business) as a result of using the marketing tool ClickFunnels. He has been featured in *Forbes* and Business Insider and on CBS and CNBC. For more information, visit eliteceos.com and www. infiniteincomebook.com/info.

CPSIA information can be obtained
at www.ICGtesting.com
Printed in the USA
BVHW070526141121
621334BV00002B/5